Servants of the THIRD WATCH

Servants of the THIRD WATCH

S.F. Fleming

Copyright © 2002 by S. F. Fleming. All rights reserved.

Printed in the United States of America

Publishing services by Selah Publishing, Arizona. The views expressed
or implied in this work do not necessarily reflect those of Selah Publishing.

ISBN- 1-58930-042-4
Library of Congress Control Number: 2001095976

Dedicated to the servants of the third watch. Some of them are mentioned in the pages of this book; countless more are serving the Lord in places around the world with little or no recognition of men. Yet, the Lord knows each of their names, and they are valuable to Him for His service. Someday all these names will be revealed for they are written in the Lamb's Book of Life.

CONTENTS

Foreword

In your hands is a book that will provide for you, and others who read it, a much-needed insight into the subject of the coming of the Lord Jesus Christ. Over the years, many books have been written on this subject based on conjecture and speculation and, in many cases, these books have been proven wrong. First Chronicles 12:32 speaks of the sons of Issachar who understood the times as to what Israel should do. Stan Fleming, the author of *Servants of the Third Watch*, functions as one of those sons of Issachar in this book.

Many people in our present generation are confused on the subject of the Second Coming. No matter what one's perspective is, there seems to be an uncertainty of when and where this coming will really take place. Part of the problem is because of a failure to grasp just where our culture is at this time.

One author points out that in every civilization and culture there are four levels that operate in a cycle. [1]The first is spiritual dominance followed by spiritual decline. This, in turn, flows down to spiritual captivity and fourth,

---

[1]William Strauss and Neil Howe, *The Fourth Turning: An Anmerican Prophecy* (Broadway Books, 1998).

spiritual ascendancy. The pattern is clear that in Israel there was spiritual dominance in the time of Joshua, followed by a time of idolatry, leading to a period of total bondage to other nations. Then, spiritual dominance would arise and the nation would again become strong. Later, we see this again in the reign of David and then Solomon where spiritual dominance was followed by decline, culminating in spiritual and national captivity. Again under Nehemiah the nation begins to rise, only to fall into further sin, resulting in four hundred years of silence until Jesus comes. The church of the book of Acts rises to spiritual dominance in its day followed later by its decline; this results in the Dark Ages which continues until the Protestant Reformation.

The author of this book believes that the American culture today is somewhere between spiritual decline and spiritual bondage or darkness. If that is the case, then how should we live? Stan Fleming gives us some great insights. We don't throw up our hands in hopelessness.

Isaiah chapter 60 states, "For behold, darkness will cover the earth, And deep darkness the peoples; But the Lord will rise upon you and His glory will appear upon you. And nations will come to your light, And kings to the brightness of your rising" (verses 2-3 NASB). As Stan develops the concept of the Third Watch, we gain the hope that at midnight the bridegroom arises. Much is being said about the harvest for today, as though what we are seeing now is the ultimate harvest. The fact is that the fields have always been white unto harvest. I believe that God is not giving us seed in the present ingathering to produce a greater harvest yet to be reaped. Rather, He is seeking to align the church and its leaders to prepare for both Jesus' return and the harvest. Various cultures are at various stages of the cycle, resulting in God working in different ways as to those cultures.

The American church or, for that matter, the Western world church, needs this book. I have personally known Stan Fleming for a number of years. His approach to the truths contained in this book are both scholarly as well as Spirit led. So many visions of future days are full of speculation and unwarranted conclusion with no base in Scripture. Stan lucidly leads us through the Word to demonstrate the authenticity of his personal vision. This is one of those books that has to be read two to three times to gain the full impact of his message.

Something drastic needs to happen in both the leadership of the American church as well as the laity. We need to learn the principles set forth in these pages. It's one thing to have a grasp of certain biblical facts; it's totally another to know how to apply those facts in a godly fashion. There may be a measure of darkness on our culture and society, but God wants to arise with His glory and is doing so here and there. We must know how to align ourselves with His purposes so as to have that light and glory come upon us personally and corporately. Read and digest these truths and get ready for both Christ's return *to* His church and His return *for* His church.

David Minor

PART ONE

THE VISION OF THE THIRD WATCH

The Vision

What do you think of when you hear the word *watch*? Most of us probably think of the little machines that hang on our wrists and keep time. "Tick, tick, tick," they count off the seconds and minutes of our lives and help to measure time. The first mention of the word *time* in the Scriptures is found in Genesis 4:3, but the concept of measuring time goes back farther to the creation of the first day and night (Genesis 1:3-5).

In our language the word *watch* has other meanings as well. We can watch the sunset or we can watch the flowers bloom. Our children grow, and we watch them with delight and surprise. There are bird watchers, people watchers, and star watchers. Watching can be something that happens in a short space of time or over a long period. We watch out for one another, which brings an aspect of precaution and safety. There is also the idea of the watchman in the watchtower. And Christians are aware that our Lord Jesus told us to watch and be ready for His return.

I have always been aware of the biblical term *watch* in regard to a certain period of time in which people might stand watch. The vision I received in the fall of 1999, however, propelled me into an investigation of the Scriptures that has given me much more to consider. I hope it will make you stop and consider it as well.

It is normally cold during the October nights in northern Idaho, and 1999 was typical. It might have seemed colder and darker than most fall seasons as we approached the new year of 2000 with the media buzzing about the Y2K computer bug and the possible surge of apocalyptic terrorist cults. Much had been on my mind as a pastor, and I probably went to sleep that particular night thinking about aspects of the ministry, as well as preparation for a leadership seminar I was to teach in the Philippines in November. I didn't know that I was to have one of those middle-of-the-night meetings with the Lord. Have you ever been partially awakened and had the spirit of the Lord speak something profound to you? It happened to me that night.

My rest was interrupted, and I awoke. As I was in that semi-conscious, dreamlike state, the Spirit of the Lord spoke to me, *"The church is entering into the third watch, the third guard."* I was shocked by the words that I heard because my thoughts were nowhere near that idea. Actually, I was just waking up and don't even remember what I was thinking, but it was nothing like that. At the same time I heard it, I was given a brief micro-second revelation of the entire Christian world from what I believe to be a heavenly perspective. That is why I refer to it as a vision; the words brought an understanding I could see in my mind.

In the Spirit, I saw the entire Christian world being ushered into a new time in history. I saw the church in the earth, not as man sometimes sees it with denominational, ethnic, and political boundaries, but rather I saw those called-out ones who serve Jesus their Lord, no matter what Christian group they are in, what race they belong to, or where they live. I felt like heaven was meekly announcing that it was time to change the watch. We were entering into the third watch.

In my spirit, I felt as though angelic bells were ringing all over creation as the church was entering into the third watch, the third guard. The vision and weight of the words soaked into my soul and sent chills up my spine. Wave upon wave of emotion swept over me as I heard the words, saw the vision, and considered what I had just experienced.

The emphasis was on the words *third watch* and *third guard*. I did not know until later the words could be synonymous. To me they were plainly spoken and gentle, yet there was a confidence in the words that this change in watch was in the process of happening. There was no anxiousness expressed in what was spoken; only anticipation that this was to be a momentous watch.

I did not know how long the process of changing the watch required; it could have been seconds or years. The depth of the vision—as brief as it was—allowed me to visualize the need for the church to do three things to prepare for this new watch: 1) fervently maintain and upgrade our watch for the return of the Lord, 2) guard the borders of Christianity against heresy, and 3) extend God's kingdom throughout the world.

In a way, the ideas of maintaining our watch, guarding our borders, and extending God's kingdom are no different than what the church was supposed to do before. However, there was in that announcement of the vision an idea that the third watch had amazing importance to it, and that now the church would do what it was supposed to do because it was in God's plan and timing for it to arise to the hour of need.

What was the third watch or third guard? I had no idea but, beginning that day, I decided to research the Bible to see if there was anything to it. I have enough prophetic experience to know that these things need to be confirmed in the Scriptures. Otherwise, the source for them could easily be our imagination, the pizza we ate, or even a demonic seed. It was a subjective experience. I did not even know if the words *third watch* were in the Bible.

I had been praying that the Lord would help me prepare for a leadership conference I had been asked to teach in the Philippines. The theme of the conference was *Preparing Leaders for the New Millennium,* and the pastor who invited me wanted the emphasis to lean toward end-time events. Thus, when I received the vision, I thought the Lord was just giving me an idea for the conference. However, there seemed to be much more to it than that. I couldn't get away from the ecstasy my soul experienced as the words were said, and I saw the church from what I thought was God's perspective.

As I explained before, the vision occurred quickly. I thought about the words for a couple of days and then decided to write them down so I would not forget them. But it took me several days to get to the point of really studying the topic in the Scriptures. As a husband, father, and pastor of a very active church in Idaho, it's all I can do to keep up with everything.

The subject of watches was not completely foreign to me. As I mentioned before, I knew the concept was mentioned in the Bible a couple of times, but it never meant anything to me. However, when I started researching the third watch, what I discovered amazed me. I not only found the topic in the Scriptures, but I also found many astonishing revelations about the whole subject that I had never read about or been taught. After an examination of these concepts, you may agree with me that this watch could prove to be profoundly significant in regard to the church in the world. As I looked deeper into the subject, I encountered many thoughts about the way Christians *are*, compared to the way we *should* be.

The message of the *third watch* became my kick-off sermon in the Philippines, and while I did minister to the pastors and leaders about certain end-time events as had been requested, my emphasis was right back on the time-proven character qualities of leadership that have led the church through the last two millennia. Why? Because we are going into the third millennium, like it or not, and we had better stand up and be prepared for what lies ahead as, one day, this generation of Christians will be called upon to give an account of what we did during this watch.

Basic End-time Views

Before continuing with the concepts derived from the vision, let us briefly consider some major Christian views regarding the return of the Lord Jesus Christ. Most theologians and Christians believe that the Bible teaches the doctrine of the Second Coming. According to Scripture, this is the blessed hope of Christians (Titus 2:13), the great event for which they long. That is not to say that this is our constant focus; that would be impossible. We must live our lives and serve the Lord until He returns. However, Christians, in general, are excited that the day will come when they can bow down before the One who saved them from their sins and who opened the way into eternal life for them.

There will be such great rejoicing that nothing in recorded history will come close to the occasion.

There are many current competing views regarding what the Bible has to say about the end times or last days and the timetable of the Lord's return. The various camps all have certain strengths and weaknesses. Each one incorporates the second return of the Lord Jesus but each has drastically different views regarding how the Bible describes it.

Three basic criteria distinguish and help define these camps. First, most of them attach the point of Jesus' return in relationship to a 1,000-year period or millennium. To some, this millennium will be a thousand years of Christ and His saints reigning on earth (Revelation 21). The following is a generalization but gets across the basic understanding of each view. *Premillennialists* believe that Jesus will return before the literal thousand years; *postmillennialists* believe that Jesus will return after the thousand years; and *amillennialists* are less literal and believe that the church is already in a symbolic millennium and that it represents whatever period of time the Lord designates until He returns.

The issue of a literal or spiritual perspective on biblical interpretation is the second major difference. For instance, the amillennialists start interpretation from a position of spiritualizing the Bible, whereas the postmillennialists and premillennialists begin interpretation from a literal perspective; it means just what it says.

The argument over a literal or spiritual view really alters final analysis. For example, if one's view of the forthcoming prophecies of the book of Revelation is that most or all of them are literal events that will happen, this leads to a different thinking than a person who surmises that the matters of Revelation are not literal but only spiritual truths for us to merely understand. The one camp is accused of spiritualizing away obvious literal events such as the seven years of tribulation, while the second camp is accused of taking everything literally, such as the 144,000 servants from the twelve tribes of Israel. This, at times, appears ridiculous.

Today, the largest group of Christians—including liberal theologians, some mainline Protestant denominations, and Roman Catholicism—is actually in the amillennial group. This is a generalization, but the basic thrust within this group is that there is no literal 1,000-year period and no seven years of tribulation. Jesus will someday return and heaven will begin with Him.

The postmillennialists take the Bible literally but they differ from premillennialists in that they think Jesus will return after a thousand years of the church's influence, bringing a golden age of Christianization to all the nations of the world. Prominent individuals such as John and Charles Wesley, Charles Spurgeon, John Calvin, Isaac Newton, George Whitfield, and many more held this view. The conviction for this theological position was given a great shaking by the onslaught of WWI and WWII, and the footing for its doctrine became almost extinct during a significant part of the twentieth century. Yet, today, various charismatics and those with a heritage of Reformed theology are once again embracing some form of this view.

The third standard for difference applies mainly to the premillennial camp and divides it into various theological groups. The distinction has to do with the seven years of tribulation spoken of in Revelation and Daniel. There is internal debate within the premillennialist camp on whether the Scriptures teach that Christ will return in the pretribulation, midtribulation, or posttribulation period.

Other groups hold such views such as the pre-wrath rapture and the partial rapture view.

Evangelicals and Pentecostals often have a premillennial viewpoint. However, once again it is important to mention that it is a generalization to say that one group is completely amillennial, premillennial, or postmillennial.

It should also be noted that a few theologians, known as ultrapreterists, embrace the view that Jesus returned in the first century around 70 A.D. at the time of the destruction of Jerusalem. While the vast majority of scholars and theologians reject this view outright, it does show the great diversity of opinion and thought on the subject.

A New Paradigm of Understanding

The major theological schools of thought about the Second Coming begin with the thousand year period of Revelation 20 and then work out their doctrine from there. Accordingly, they then come to a possible approximate time for the Lord to return.

Yet, what if the answers to some of our deepest questions about the timing of the Lord are really much simpler? We know that Jesus used many parables to explain about the end times, as well as teachings about the signs of the time near the point of His return. Of these doctrines, there is one often overlooked parable that is quite significant for the servant of the Lord in the timetable of working through God's plan. The parable I am referring to is that of the watching servants.

If the concept of the third watch found in the parable of the watching servants is correct, it gets outside the biblical box that these other camps have created regarding the coming of the Lord, and it pioneers a new paradigm to work from. The third watch does not necessarily violate these other views, but it does add a whole new dimension of understanding that may ultimately shift the emphasis and challenge *alarmist* ideas.

The Basic Point

As we investigate the topic of the third watch, it will become apparent that we live in a unique time in history. This is the midnight hour of the third watch in conjunction with that of the third day. Never before has this occurred and in a few decades it will be over. There are strategic opportunities for the church to embrace and the need for transition in a church that is changing the watch. We must heed the call to be servants *and* watchers.

Jesus said some very important things about the third watch and those who serve, and we will investigate those things in future chapters. What are our responsibilities as servants of the third watch? What should our attitude be? What does the Bible say about the midnight hour of the church and Jesus coming as a thief in the night?

Ultimately, I hope the reader will perceive this: We probably have more reason to expect the return of Jesus Christ than any other generation that has ever lived, but we also have more need than any other generation to not have an *escapist* or *alarmist* attitude. We must serve, we must be mature, we must be strong, we must be patient, and we must raise up the next generation to serve God with all of their hearts!

I have divided this book into several parts. Part One considers the biblical reasoning behind the concept of the third watch and other connecting themes. Part Two emphasizes the need for individual Christians to be servants and watchers. We look, but do we really see? Part Three focuses on the responsibility of the transitioning church in the third watch. It also gets outside the box and considers others that are watching the church. Each chapter begins with a brief biography of servants in various places who are serving the Lord and watching for His return.

QUESTIONS: FOR STUDY, REVIEW AND DISCUSSION

1. The word *watch* has many meanings. What are some of them?

2. Have you ever experienced a vision that you felt was from the Lord? Did you go to the Bible to confirm it? Did the Bible confirm it?

3. What are the basic differences between amillennialists, premillennialists, and postmillennialists in regard to the thousand years and interpretation?

4. The timing of the tribulation has caused various groupings in the premillennialist camp. What are some of the different views on this subject?

5. What new paradigm of understanding does the third watch suggest?

The Parable of the Watching Servants

Pastor Peter Mayyam and his wife, Loreta, watch for the Lord in the Philippines. Peter's grandfather was an influential and popular high pagan priest who was very involved in occultism, and it would have been easy for Peter to follow in those steps and ignore the calling of the Lord on his life. Yet, Peter chose the Lord, and from his humble dwelling in Baguio, Philippines, he prayerfully watches. He looks not only for the return of the Lord but also for the leading of the Holy Spirit in his life. The Lord has used him to start over thirty churches in the mountainous regions in little towns and among tribal people. The church he pastors in La Trinidad holds biannual conferences for pastors from around the country. After times of praise and worship, the sessions at the conference often center on sharing the gospel with the lost, keeping passion for God alive, remembering that the Lord is coming again soon, and living life in such a way that it brings glory to Jesus Christ.

My Discovery

The first thing I learned in my search through the Scriptures was that Jesus Himself taught us about the significance of the night watches. Indeed! He even specifically emphasized the second and third watches. As I taught the concepts of the third watch to the many Filipino pastors gathered at Peter's church near Baguio, I noticed that they were as amazed as I with this parable that seems to have gone unnoticed by theologians who wrestle with the timing of the Lord's return. Notice what Jesus says in the following parable about the timing of the master's return and the appropriate attitude of his servants:

> Let your waist be girded and your lamps burning; and you yourselves be like men who wait for their master, when he will return from the wedding, that when he comes and knocks they may open to him immediately. Blessed are those servants whom the master, when he comes, will find watching. Assuredly, I say to you that he will gird himself and have them sit down to eat, and will come and serve them. And if he should come in the second watch, or *come in the third watch*, and find them so, blessed are those servants
>
> LUKE 12:35-38, EMPHASIS ADDED.

The Word *Watch*

In my college days, I took scuba diving and needed a diving watch. However, as with most college students, I had little money for expensive watches. My friend Phil, also in the class, paid thirty dollars for his waterproof watch, but got water in it after the first dive. My brother had a two-hundred-dollar waterproof watch with every gadget imaginable. One day, while he was in the shower with his watch safely on the counter, it got water inside simply through condensation. So you can imagine how good I felt about the purchase of my seven-dollar waterproof scuba diving watch that could submerse to thirty feet, go in showers, and even be dropped on concrete without any defect.

Of course, the word *watch* in the parable above has little to do with a wristwatch, but just as there are many types and qualities of wristwatches, there are many meanings of the word *watch* in the Scriptures. There are three Greek nouns and up to five verbs that can be rendered into some form of the English word *watch*. For example, the Greek noun *phulake* is used in Luke 2:8 to describe how the shepherds kept watch or guarded their sheep by night. In Acts 12:10, however, the same word is used as a military term for guarding or keeping watch and is rendered *ward*. In this verse, we read about an angel leading Peter past the first and second wards or *guard-posts*. The Greek noun for *watch* can also signify a period of time or a specific division of hours. There are various Greek verb forms as well, the most obvious meaning the action of vigilant observation.

The Old Testament Hebrew words for *watch* somewhat parallel the New Testament Greek meanings. However, in the Old Testament we can also find it compounded in the words *watchman* and *watchtower*. These watchmen were literal guards in their guard towers watching over the city and watching out for enemy attack.

There was also the prophetic sense of the words. For instance, the prophet, Habakkuk, stood on prophetic *watch* in his watchtower (Habakkuk 2:1), and God told Ezekiel to be a "watchman for the house of Israel" (Ezekiel 3:17). Today, there are prophetic people whom God uses as watchmen in churches and communities to warn His people against danger. If the watchmen fall to sleep, the people will perish!

Another interesting way the word is used in the Old Testament is in the word *watchers,* referring to angels in the fourth chapter of the book of Daniel. These angelic visitors apparently watch people, which might make those who are paranoid say, "Aha, I knew I felt someone watching me," and then proceed to freak out. However, God usually sends angels for the good of people (Hebrews 1:14). We'll consider the topic of these watchers later on in Chapter Ten. (Yet, who knows? Perhaps it was the unseen hand of an angel that caused my nimble fingers to falter, thus dropping my seven-dollar scuba diving watch—the one of which I had deliberately and continuously boasted about to my brother and friend—onto the shag carpet where it exploded into a dozen pieces. My pride was suddenly silenced.)

Another concept of the word *watch* is the idea of "keeping watch." This goes back to the Garden of Eden. The Hebrew word *shamar* means, "to keep, tend, watch over, or retain." It was a part of the responsibility God gave to Adam. In Genesis 2:15, God told Adam to *keep* or *watch over* the garden. Unfortunately, he shirked his responsibility when it came to obeying the command of the Lord in regard to the tree of the knowledge of good and evil. This first watch, or keeping of the garden, was breached when Adam not only observed Eve eat of the forbidden fruit without his protest (Genesis 3:6), but then he, too, transgressed the watch by partaking in the same breach of the Lord's command. How many times do spouses or loved ones simply stand by today as someone they care for ruins his or her life by feeding on things that God has forbidden when a small word of warning or exhortation from them might change the entire outcome?

Now that we have considered various usages of the word, let's come back to how it is actually used in the parable of the watching servants. In this story, it implies vigilant watching and guarding, but it also refers to a specific division of hours, the second and third watches of the night.

Old and New Testament Time Divisions

The divisions of time were different for the watches in the Old Testament and the New Testament. Ancient Israel had three watches of four hours each, while the Israel of Jesus' time used the Roman system of four watches of three hours each. Numerous commentators, as well as Thomas Nelson Publishers, verify the accuracy of the following biblical watch systems.[1]

Below is a comparison between the two measuring systems used for night watches during the time of ancient Israel in the Old Testament and that of Jesus in the New Testament:

Ancient Israel	Jesus' time
1st 6 P.M.-10 P.M. sunset to midnight)	1st 6 P.M.-9 P.M. sunset to evening)
2nd 10 P.M. - 2 A.M. (midnight to cockcrow)	2nd 9 P.M. - 12 A.M. (evening to midnight)
3rd 2 A.M. - 6 A.M. (cockcrow to sunrise)	3rd 12 A.M. - 3 A.M. (midnight to cockcrow)
	4th 3 A.M. - 6 A.M. (cockcrow to sunset)

---

[1] Thomas Nelson Publishers, well known for Bibles and teaching aids, explains the watch system of New Testament days being at three hour intervals beginning at 6:00 P.M., 9:00 p.m., midnight, and 3:00 A.M. Zondervan uses this same time system in their Bibles, but in their *Pictorial Bible Dictionary*, they describe the watches as being at two-and-a-half-hour intervals beginning at 9:30 P.M., midnight, 2:30 A.M., and 5:00 A.M. However, well-respected commentators such as Adam Clarke and Matthew Henry subscribe to the three-hour intervals beginning at 6:00 P.M. This makes more sense since the New Testament writers seemed to indicate events by naming hours that would be at three-hour intervals (see Matthew 27:45; Mark 15:25; John 19:14; Acts 1:15).

What time is it for you right now? How would you know if you didn't have a wristwatch? You might look at the clock on the wall, the alarm clock next to your bed, the clock on the kitchen stove, or on your computer. We have clocks everywhere that tell us what time it is. We don't want to be late because we are such a time-oriented society. But what if they were all gone? Zap! They disappeared! What then? Well, you could look outside. Is it dark or light? How high is the sun or moon in the sky? Humankind has always been interested in tracking the time, but didn't always have the power of modern science to do so. However, they used those things at their disposal to keep the best time possible.

The Lord Jesus didn't use a wristwatch, but He was well acquainted with how time was kept in His day. He also understood how it was kept in ancient Israel. Because this has a bearing on the amount of hours in the third watch, one might ask, "Which system did Jesus use when telling parables?" The answer is not hard to find. Jesus used the Roman system of the four watches as indicated by another parable found in Mark 13:35:

> Watch therefore, for you do not know when the master of the house is coming—1) in the evening, 2) at midnight, 3) at the crowing of the rooster, or 4) in the morning (numbers added).

This Scripture above is divided into four distinct time slots and appears parallel to the New Testament Roman night watch system. Notice how the Roman structure shown below parallels with what Jesus spoke in Mark 13:35:

Roman System	Mark 13:35
1st watch: 6 P.M. - 9 P.M. (sunset to evening)	"in the evening"
2nd watch: 9 P.M. - 12 A.M. (evening to midnight)	"at midnight"
3rd watch: 12 A.M. - 3 A.M. (midnight to cockcrow)	"at the crowing of the rooster"
4th watch 3 A.M. - 6 A.M. (cockcrow to sunset)	"in the morning"

What Does This Mean?

Our whole way of life today would be stymied if we set our schedule around sundown, sunset, the crowing of a rooster, or the blowing of trumpets. Setting curfews for kids would be hard if you said, "Be home by midnight," and they responded, "Sure thing, Dad. When is that?"

However, in regard to the parable, we must realize that Jesus was expressing an important concept to us, as He did with all of His teaching. If we accept that Jesus referred to four watches in the natural when telling His parables, then the third watch begins at 12:00 A.M. (midnight) and ends at 3:00 A.M. (cockcrow). "Okay, the third watch begins at our midnight hour and ends at 3:00 A.M.," someone might say. "So what? Why is it important?"

To answer that question, we must remember that the Lord Jesus hid important messages of moral and religious truth within His parables. When He taught this parable of the watching servants in Luke 12, He certainly knew the hours involved in the watch time system. His purpose was not to give the hearers a lesson on a typical twenty-four-day period or when a master might return from a wedding festival. Rather, His primary objective was to help us better understand the general timing of the Lord's return and our responsibility as servants. That is what this parable is about, and that is what makes it important.

The fact that this is about the Lord's return and not just a nice story about a master and his servants becomes even more obvious as we read past the parable of the watching servants and on through the next one of the watching house-holder. This adds information that Luke wished the reader to understand about the subject. Notice the warning in the next parable.

> But know this, that if the master of the house had known what hour the thief would come, he would have watched and not allowed his house to be broken into. Therefore you also be ready, for the Son of Man is coming at an hour you do not expect .
>
> LUKE 12:39-40

One night, years ago, someone broke into our church building, vandalized things for no apparent reason, and stole items from the desks of students in our Christian day school. One of the things stolen from my daughter's desk was an award she had received for Christian character. It was a small clock within plastic mounted on a marble base, and it meant a lot to her since the other students had voted to give the award to her. The thief unscrewed the marble base and took only the clock in plastic. Things were also taken from other desks and the church. This wasn't the only time we had had a break in and, each time, we felt violated. Someone had come and done something he should not have done. Eventually, we got wise and put an alarm on the building. It's amazing how well a simple alarm deters a thief!

The parable in Luke, however, puts a strange twist on the subject of thievery as this warning is about the Son of Man coming unexpectedly—the "Son of Man" being one of the titles for the Lord Jesus Christ. He is also referred to in other scriptures as "a thief in the night."

The point of this is simple. The position of these verses, following the parable of the watching servants, adds clarification that this is about the second coming of the Lord Jesus Christ.

Of course, this last parable says that the *hour* of His return will be unexpected. Other passages say that no one knows the day nor hour of His return (see Matthew 24:36,44; 25:13). Mark writes more of a general theme saying, "Take heed, watch and pray; for you do not know when the time is" (Mark 13:33). Because the Bible makes it plain that no one is privy to the actual twenty-four-hour day or sixty-minute hour that Jesus will return, these verses can be taken quite literally. Yet, Jesus did tell His followers that we could know the approximate season (Matthew 24:32-33) of His return based, upon end-time events. In many of His teachings, He explained what the conditions of the world would be just prior to His return. Furthermore, He gave us the hint of a timetable with regard to the night watches.

Questions: For Study, Review and Discussion

1. Read and meditate upon the parable of the watching servants found in Luke 12:35-38. What things stand out to you?

2. Consider some of the biblical concepts of the word *watch*. For instance, what does the Hebrew word *shamar* mean? What was Adam's responsibility and how did he handle it?

3. Discuss the difference between the Old and New Testament time divisions for the Jews. How many night watches did each have? Which one did Jesus use in daily life and in teaching? What time did the third watch of Jesus' time begin and end?

4. What primary objective did Jesus have in telling the parable of watching servants?

5. Luke placed the parable of the watching householder (verses 39-40) directly after the one of the watching servants. What are their similarities? What point do you think Luke makes by placing them next to each other?

THE WATCHES OF THE NIGHT

Andrew Coodelya watches for the Lord from Novorrossik, Russia, on the Black Sea. Today, Andrew is an electrician and attends a Pentecostal Holiness Church. Formerly, he was an officer in the Red Guard before the Berlin Wall came down. After the Army, he needed money to support his wife and two children in this poverty-stricken country, so he began running with a criminal gang. After two years, his life was a mess. He was bedridden with triple pneumonia. His wife, Irena—tired of his affairs and his life of crime—mockingly threw a New Testament at him one day and told him it was his only hope. Andrew picked it up. After three months of reading it, he repented first of adultery, then smoking, and then drinking. After praying to accept the Lord, he was converted and healed. The next week he attended a church that gave him another New Testament with the name and address of a church in Idaho, United States, printed on the first page and he wrote a letter to that address asking for help. It was our church. When I received his letter, I could barely read it as he knew no English and had used an English dictionary to compose it. We helped Andrew and now, years later, he and his whole family are Christians and serve the Lord in the oppressed societies of Russia and their native country of Ukraine.

A Thousand Years As a Watch

A new soldier was on sentry duty one night at the main gate of a military post. His orders were clear: No car was to enter unless it had a special sticker on the windshield. Near midnight, as he was keeping his watch of the gate, a big Army car drove up with a general seated in the back. The sentry said, "Halt, who goes there?" The chauffeur said, "General Wheeler." The sentry replied, "I'm sorry, I can't let you through. You've got to have a sticker on the windshield." The general ignored the guard and said to the chauffeur, "Drive on." The sentry warned again, "Hold it. You really can't come through. I have orders to shoot if you try driving in without a sticker." The general, in an agitated voice said, "Corporal, I'm telling you to drive on." At this point, the sentry walked up to the rear window and said, "Pardon me, General. I'm really kind of new at all of this. Who do I shoot first, you or the driver?"

A new soldier on watch might not know that generals may sometimes bend the rules as they are often the ones who make those rules. If the soldier had been a regular guard at that gate, he probably would have recognized the general and there would have been no problem. Experience as a sentry on watch duty has its advantages. A solo novice on duty probably does not happen much at military installations; hopefully, it does not happen much in the church either.

Yet, there comes a time to change the guard, to change the watch. The expertise of the watchmen is dictated by the importance of what is guarded. Consider, for instance, the stately change of guard at Buckingham Palace. Their movements are precise and impeccable.

As the global church changes the guard, I wonder if the movements will be as precise and impeccable! Probably so, when we see how the hand of God has been involved as it would most likely be the movement of the Holy Spirit making the adjustment. If the church is entering the third watch, then possibly a strategic repositioning is going on by the Holy Spirit, in order to bring a new vanguard of watchmen ministries to their posts in preparation for the events that may occur during this watch.

The transition into the third watch is much more meaningful, however, than simply a new set of watchmen. *All* Christians are called to watch. Yet, this new watch is not just about people watching; it is about a new time in history. New things are going to happen. New challenges will face the church. There will be a new attitude in the church, a paradigm shift in outlook. As a person's attitude or outlook is changed according to the time of day, so the church will transition into a change of outlook. We have entered into the third watch, into the midnight hour, and thus must be on guard for those things that will approach the gates. We should call upon all of the expertise of Christian history to perform our duty well.

Someone might say, "That sounds lofty and grand if we *really* are entering the third watch, but how do we know from Scripture that we are actually in this watch? Perhaps we are still in the first watch, second watch, or have gone ahead into the fourth watch." Or he might say, "Stan, that was a nice vision you had about the third watch but give me some Scripture that supports the idea that we are now in that spiritual timeframe." Fair enough. Let's consider it.

I must admit that when I first had the vision and began investigating the Bible, I had these same questions. Then I came across the following two verses with a connection I had not understood before. The first is very familiar, while the second is rarely considered.

> But, beloved do not forget this one thing, that with the Lord one day is as a thousand years, and a thousand years as one day (2 Peter 3:8).

> For a thousand years in Your sight are like yesterday when it is past, and *like a watch in the night* (Psalm 90:4, emphasis added).

The verse in 2 Peter 3 actually finds its roots in Psalm 90, which was a prayer written by Moses. Both of these verses give us insight into how the Lord reckons time. Both chapters refer to the flood and various aspects of God's timing in regard to divine judgment; both emphasize the eternity of God compared to the temporary nature of men and creation; and both imply the need for patience of the saints for the return of the Lord. Of course, Moses was possibly referring to a return of the Lord's presence and favor upon Israel in the desert, whereas Peter was literally referring to the second coming of Jesus Christ. Peter says that "the day of the Lord will come as a thief in the night" (2 Peter 3:10) but it will be in God's timing because He is patient with people, not wanting anyone to perish "but that all should come to repentance" (verse 9).

There is a side to these time comparisons that is metaphorical but also quite literal. For a metaphorical example, consider the housewife who gets the kids off to school, prays, reads the Bible, cleans the house, does laundry, cooks, goes to the store, counsels a friend, makes a budget, mows the lawn, prepares a Sunday school lesson, takes the kids to soccer practice, greets her husband affectionately as he comes home from work, serves dinner, and reads a bedtime story to her children. As she wearily climbs into bed at night, she might feel like it's been a thousand years since morning. However, the opposite is also true. When the kids are grown, the dog has died, and mid-age bulge has set in, she feels that the years have flown by. It seems only yesterday that her children were young! It passed so fast, like a day or watch in the night.

This is one sense we get from both Moses' and Peter's words. But there is a literal aspect to what they say as well. Regarding the literal characteristic, the verse in Peter is quoted by Christians to illustrate that a thousand years by men's standards correlates to a single day by the Lord's measurement, or vice versa. However, what is normally not considered is that a thousand years in the Lord's sight is also like *a watch in the night.*

Comparing a Thousand Years to a Day of the Lord

The simplest way to understand this is to take a literal interpretation of Scripture in regard to 2 Peter 3:8. If we believe that a single day of the Lord is worth a thousand years of men, and if God created mankind only 6,000 years ago, then this would be six days in the Lord's timing. We would then be entering the seventh day or seven thousandth year. This is the day of God's rest according to Genesis 2:2-3 and, according to some theologians, the beginning of the thousand-year millennial reign of righteousness referred to in Revelation, chapter 20. With these things in mind, we can then see much significance to the current millennium.

In conjunction with this consideration is the aspect that Jesus came at the time of transition between the fourth and fifth day, or at the end of the 4,000-year period and the beginning of the 5,000-year period. This is significant because He taught so much about His rising on the third day, which literally happened at His resurrection. However, some think, with good reason, that He was also giving spiritual insight to the number of thousand-year-intervals that would pass before His second coming. Well, approximately 2,000 years have passed since His birth, so we are now in the third thousand-year-period (or the third day since Jesus' birth).

Jesus said, "Destroy this temple, and in three days I will raise it up" (John 2:19). This literally happened. Add to this what the prophet Hosea said, "After two days He will revive us; On the third day He will raise us up, that we may live in His sight" (Hosea 6:2), and we get some profound implications for the age of the church. Is this indicating that the Lord will raise up His true temple, the church, into her glorified state in this day (this millennium)?

Basically, there are two starting points to reckon biblical-day periods or thousand-year periods, one being the creation of man and the other the birth of Christ. For those who take the Scriptures literally (and I do), we are entering the seventh day (or seven thousandth year) from the creation of man, as well as the third day (or three thousandth year) since Christ's birth.

Comparing a Thousand Years to a Watch in the Night

Psalm 90:4 indicates that God also uses the concept of a night watch to illustrate a thousand years by man's timetable. Thus, we are not spiritually entering into a new day only, but also into a new watch.

We are in the beginning of the third watch (the third thousand-year period) since the time of Jesus. One amazing aspect of our particular time in history is that because the third watch begins at midnight, as we have already seen, in actuality, it is the beginning of a new day as well. It is the seventh day since the creation of man and the third day since Jesus' birth, but it is also uniquely the third watch of the new day.

Jesus used the parable of the watching servants to announce that the Lord might return in the second or third watch. So if we reckon time beginning from Jesus' birth, the first and second watches are both over. Therefore, we must be entering the third watch, the third thousandth year since His birth.

We are entering the third day but also the third watch. The concepts are both synonymous for a thousand-year period, but it is amazing that we have now entered the midnight hour of the third watch as well as the beginning of the third day.

In the next section, we will look at the significant things that happened during the watches in the last day of Jesus before His death. Then we will look specifically at the events of the third watch and how they relate to His resurrection.

Significant Events Surrounding Jesus' Death and Resurrection

What is the most painful thing you have experienced? I think the most physically painful thing I have ever felt happened about seventeen years ago. While on summer break from serving as a minister of education in our church's Christian school, I was doing some house painting to earn some extra money. One moment I was painting the outside of an apartment complex, and thirty minutes later I was writhing in pain and being rushed into an emergency hospital unit with a kidney stone. Thank heavens for modern hospitals and medication! I was told that I would have lived because the stone would have passed eventually, but the pain was so intense I thought I was going to die. Even through the injection of pain medication, I could feel the edges of the ache. (I have since been told that kidney stones are the closest thing a man can feel which compares to a woman having a baby. Sorry, ladies!)

There is other pain also besides physical distress. There is the emotional anguish of rejection and betrayal, and the mental pain that comes from being mocked and ridiculed. Pain equals suffering no matter how it inflicts its victim.

Each of us has a threshold of pain that we can endure, whether it be physical, emotional, or mental. At some point, we pass out, check out, or hope to move out to escape the pain. On the other hand, there comes a certain level of pain that when reached can get no worse. Even if more pain is inflicted, the victim has already experienced ultimate anguish and can feel no greater level of hurt.

This must be the level of pain that our Lord Jesus reached when He suffered in His passion on behalf of all men. We get a glimpse of this suffering when we read the account in the Gospels and other Scriptures such as Isaiah 52-53 and Psalm 22.

Hebrews 12:2 tells us that Jesus "for the joy that was set before Him endured the cross." I am so glad that He could see past His suffering and pain into the future of lives transformed as a result of His death, burial, and resurrection. As Isaiah said, "He bore the sin of many, and made intercession for the transgressors" (Isaiah 53:12).

Jesus was crucified at about 9:00 A.M. by our standard of time, having been beaten, scourged, mocked, pricked by thorns, and pierced by nails. He then hung on the cross for six grueling hours until 3:00 P.M. at which time He cried, "My God, My God, why have you forsaken Me?" Then He yielded up His spirit into the Father's hands (Matthew 27:46-50).

As I was studying all of this with respect to the third watch, I suddenly realized that a lot of significant events happened either at three-hour intervals or within recognized watches. It's similar to buying a new car. Suddenly, it seems like everyone you see is driving the same make and model. Well, since I became interested in the watches of the night, things popped out at me in all the Gospels about the watches with respect to Jesus.

I'm not trying to read something into Scripture that isn't there, but this information was so interesting, I wanted to pass it on to the reader. I have listed a number of events that occurred in the last twenty-four hour period of Jesus' life. These occurrences happened either at exact three-hour intervals or during one of the watches. There is enough specific scriptural information or internal textual data to give a general timeframe or watch in which these events most likely transpired. For example, remember that the word *evening*, as we discussed in chapter two, means the first watch, thus when it is used in Matthew 26:20 in conjunction with the Last Supper, it confirms in what watch this meal transpired.

I admit that the time elements for Gethsemane and the betrayal of Judas are only educated guesses, as there is no specific information given. However, we do have some facts that make these suggestions practical. We know, for instance, that the Last Supper took awhile and this would have filled up the first watch. We also know that the events at Gethsemane took some time and would have filled the second watch.

You probably know the story. Jesus went with Peter, James, and John a short distance from the other disciples, in order to pray. He encouraged these three disciples to pray with Him those final hours, but they kept falling asleep. Matthew 26:40 indicates that the first prayer watch was one hour. There were three intervals in which Jesus went away alone to pray, and if each interval lasted about an hour, then this brought the time close to midnight when Judas betrayed Him.

Furthermore, we know that much happened after Jesus was betrayed but before the rooster crowed which shamed Peter and announced the fourth watch (Matthew 26:75). Look at the following list of events and the time they occurred.

Time	Event	Scripture Reference
1st watch	Last Supper	Matthew 26:20; Mark 14:17
2nd watch	Jesus prayed in Gethsemane	Matthew 26:36-44
Around midnight	Jesus was betrayed	Matthew 26: 44-56
3rd watch	Peter's denial, Jesus before Caiaphas	Matthew 26:57-75
4th watch	Jesus before Pilate, then Herod	Luke 22:63 - 23:12
6:00 A.M.[2]	Jesus again before Pilate	John 19:14
9:00 A.M.	Jesus is crucified	Mark 15:25

----

[2] The correlating times offered in John 19:14 ("sixth hour"), Mark 15:26 ("third hour"), and Matthew 27:45 or Luke 23:44 ("the sixth

Noon	3 hours of darkness	Matthew 27:45; Luke 23:44
3:00 P.M.	Jesus died on the cross	Matthew 27:46

Notice that a lot happened to Jesus during the last four night watches before He was crucified. These events began with the Last Supper and went on through prayer in Gethsemane, betrayal, denial, trial, and judgment. The first two watches showed His anticipation of the suffering He would endure; the last two watches began that suffering.

At the beginning of the third watch, the emotional pain of Jesus began through the betrayal of Judas, the abandonment and rejection of His closest friends, and the denial of Peter. Then came the physical torment as He received beatings, whippings, and finally crucifixion.

Now consider this: Jesus was betrayed near midnight beginning the third watch; however, He would rise from the dead quite possibly during the third watch, a mere forty-eight to fifty-one hours later, triumphing over death, rejection, betrayal, and denial. How do we know this? Let's assess it.

The Possibility of the Resurrection in the Third Watch

---

hour until the ninth hour") may seem confusing at first, but they become clear when one understands the Roman and Jewish time system of that day. The "sixth hour" in John 19:14 means six hours from midnight and the formal end of their night watch. From this point, the counting begins new. So the "third hour" in Mark 15:25 is three hours after sunrise or equivalent to our 9:00 A.M. and the other ascending times of "sixth hour" and "ninth hour" found in Matthew 27:45 and Luke 23:44 correspond to our noon and 3:00 P.M.

Shortly after Jesus' death, His body was taken off the cross, dressed in burial garments, and lovingly placed in the tomb of his friend Joseph. This opened the door for one of the greatest events in history—the resurrection of the Son of God.

Today, we honor Jesus' death on Good Friday before Easter Sunday because most scholars believe this is the day Scripture indicates He died. If that is so, and we know that He died at 3:00 P.M., it was a mere thirty-three hours later that began the midnight hour introducing the first day of the new week.

Jesus, most likely, was not dead nor in the tomb for three full days (seventy-two hours) as we sometimes imagine today. When the Hebrews said *three days*, it could indicate either full days or parts of days—the same as when we might say *a couple of days from now* which means a varying amount of days and an uncertain amount of hours. For example, it is about 4 P.M. as I am writing this. Suppose someone in my congregation called me right now and said, "Pastor, I have something important to tell you, but I am leaving town and will be back on the third day. Would it be all right if I call you when I get back?" I give my consent and look forward to the call. Now, consider this. Tonight passes, as well as tomorrow. The time goes through tomorrow night past midnight and into the next day—the third day! I go to sleep, thinking that tomorrow my friend will call. If the phone interrupts my sleep at one or two o'clock in the morning—because the individual just flew in and couldn't wait to tell me the good news—I might yawn and complain, but I also must confess that I did give the permission, and it *is* the third day.

Now let's consider what we can deduce from the Gospels about when Jesus might have risen from the dead. Although there is no specific time mentioned, there are certainly several strong clues.

First, it was obviously on the third day. We know this because even Jesus told us that it would happen in three days (see Mark 14:58; John 2:19). So, it was sometime on that third day.

Second, the evidence of the empty tomb indicates that it happened sometime prior to sunrise. All four Gospels give an account of the discovery of the empty tomb sometime near dawn. Matthew 28:1 says it was about dawn; both Mark 16:2 and Luke 24:1 say it was "very early in the morning"; and John 20:1 says "early, while it was still dark." Since dawn is sometime before sunrise, then the discovery was during the fourth watch. Remember that sunrise was about 6:00 A.M. in the Roman time system that the Jews used. It was the end of the fourth watch, so the resurrection happened sometime prior to that.

Finally, the word "early" (*proi* in the Greek), mentioned in Mark and John, suggests that the discovery of the empty tomb occurred nearer the beginning of the fourth watch than around the end. The indicator is found in John 18:28 which tells of Jesus being led from Caiaphas to Pilate for the first time. The same word "early" is used in John 18:27 after Peter denied Jesus for the third time and the rooster crowed. There are different Greek words for "early." John uses *proi* to indicate a time right after the rooster crows.

Have you ever had a neighbor who owned a rooster? If so, you know that it begins crowing when it is still dark. My wife, Kathleen, and I once lived next to an older couple who emigrated from Russia. They brought their rural customs with them, including the idea of owning a rooster in the middle of town. I remember waking up night after night to the sound of "cock-a-doodle-do, cock-a-doodle-do." Kathleen and I schemed of killing that rooster, but it was impossible without offending our neighbors.

Since the rooster crowing signals the end of the third watch and beginning of the fourth, and since this same word, *proi*, is used to indicate at what time Jesus' empty tomb was discovered, it strongly suggests that the actual resurrection was earlier, during the third watch.

Different views exist about the timing of the resurrection. This is because we are examining biblical accounts written almost 2,000 years ago by authors who were emphasizing different aspects of the resurrection.

For instance, from Matthew's account, one might argue that the resurrection occurred during the fourth watch near dawn. This story in Matthew 28 shows Mary Magdalene and Mary approaching the tomb at the beginning of dawn, feeling a great earthquake, and then seeing an angel who announces the Lord's resurrection. But are the earthquake and the angel's announcement of Christ's resurrection a clear indicator that the resurrection happened during the fourth watch? I don't think so. The earthquake described in Matthew 28:2 seems to be the result of the angel of the Lord descending from heaven and rolling back the stone from the door of the tomb, rather than Jesus rising from the dead. *The opening of the tomb was not for the benefit of Jesus getting out of it but for those who came to look into the emptiness of it.* Nothing is said here about the resurrection occurring at that time.

Adding the other Gospel accounts—especially the one in the book of John—seems to indicate that the angel's announcement to Mary was actually during her second visit to the empty tomb. The details of John, chapter 20, show us clearly that Mary discovered the empty tomb upon her first time "early, while it was still dark." She then ran and told the disciples. Peter and John bolted to the tomb, investigated it, and left, then Mary returned to the tomb. This all took some time!

According to John 20:13, it was during Mary's second visit, as she stood by the tomb and wept, that angelic visitors declared the Lord's resurrection to her. After this, she was privileged to be the first to see the resurrected Lord. Therefore, unless she saw and heard angels twice, her actual discovery of the empty tomb the first time was closer to the beginning of the fourth watch. The resurrection happened prior to this, so the actuality of it occurring in the third watch is strong.

Whether it occurred in the third or fourth watch, however, it was certainly still dark and during the night when it happened. I suppose it would be nicer to think that Jesus triumphed over death just as the first light of the sun cast the dawn on the face of the land near Jerusalem. This has a romantic flavor to it. But let us not forget that a star shone down over the manger where He was born at night. Much of His earthly ministry took place during moonlight hours as He walked in gardens and taught, or ate meals with sinners, or prayed in the mountains. It was in the fourth watch of the night that He was seen walking on the waters of Galilee testing the faith of His disciples (Matthew 14:25). It was also during the night watches that He was betrayed by Judas, denied by Peter, tried by Caiaphas, and beaten by soldiers. Even when he died at 3:00 P.M., the earth and sun had already experienced supernatural darkness for three hours. So it should not really be too difficult to believe that He rose from the dead during the night watches. Neither should it be too perplexing for us to comprehend that He will come a second time from heaven, and it might very well be in the nighttime third watch of the Christian world.

CHAPTER THREE

Questions: For Study, Review and discussion

1. Read 2 Peter 3:8 and Psalm 90:4. Who wrote these verses? To what does each compare a thousand years of the Lord?

2. Discuss the above verses, both from an allegorical and literal perspective. Explain how these might be viewed allegorically. If they both are taken literally, why is it possible that we have entered both the third day and the third watch?

3. Consider the events that transpired in Jesus' life prior to crucifixion. Are there a couple that stand out to you? What happened in the third watch?

4. How many days was Jesus in the grave? How many actual hours was he dead?

5. What evidence shows that the discovery of the empty tomb was around the beginning of the fourth watch? How many times did Mary visit the tomb on the first day of the resurrection? Which Scriptures prove this?

CHAPTER FOUR

THE MIDNIGHT HOUR OF THE CHURCH

Pastor Robert and Kathyrn Baxter watch for the Lord from Paris, France. The Baxters were called by God to go to France from the United States and plant churches. This they have been successfully doing despite the anti-Christian climate in the country. They have a great love for the French people, as well as a burden to see the fires of revival spread throughout that country once again. Robert, a student of French history, knows that the Holy Spirit has impacted France many times throughout the centuries. But today, non-Catholic churches in France are normally considered cults and come under great scrutiny by socialistic government authorities. Many French people are Catholic in name only and never go to church at all. All of Europe is currently considered a place of great spiritual darkness. Yet, in certain pockets the light of Christ is shining forth and people's lives are being transformed by the love and power of God. The Baxters have experienced many miraculous events in order to even be where they are now located. Their church plants are growing, people are being touched, a certain amount of acceptance and credibility has been attained for them even in the eyes of unbelievers, and they are seeing a unity grow among the Christian pastors in Paris. Add to this, recent citywide crusades in which thousands were saved or ministered to, and it has brought joy, hope, and expectancy for the moving power of the Holy Spirit in the future of France.

As a Thief in the Night

I always thought Cary Grant was a fine actor. He could play a role so well that even if he portrayed a creep, you still liked the guy. That's how it was when he played the part of a jewel thief in *To Catch a Thief*. I remember rooting for him as he was dodging the law and apprehending another robber, a young female. In the end, it was like he was wearing a badge and white hat, and just being a good guy—a good thief.

Is there such a thing as a good thief?   The answer is yes, because Jesus portrays Himself as one. It's strange to think of Jesus as a thief, but a book has been written and a movie made entitled *A Thief in the Night,* referring to how Jesus said He would come the second time (see Matthew 24:42-44; Luke 12:39-40). Jesus will certainly be the good guy!

In Chapter Two, we examined Luke 12:39-40 and emphasized it as a warning from Jesus that a thief comes unexpectedly. The concept of Jesus coming as a thief in the night was further purported by Paul, Peter, and John in the following verses:

> The day of the Lord comes as a thief in the night (1 Thessalonians 5:2).
> The day of the Lord will come as a thief in the night (2 Peter 3:10).
> If you will not watch, I will come upon you as a thief (Revelation 3:3).
> Behold, I am coming as a thief. Blessed is he who watches... (Revelation 16:15).

Notice that both the verses written by Paul to the Thessalonians and by Peter compare the thief to the actual *day* Jesus will come, whereas John, in the book of Revelation, quotes the Lord as saying that *He* is the thief. Both views are interesting as one focuses on a time—a day—in which all things will change, while the other emphasizes the Person coming, by whom people will be startled and caught unaware.

What will happen when Jesus returns? The answer that people give to this question depends on their end-time theology. There are four views. Those who hold to the premillennial view think the rapture will occur at this time and Christians will be taken out of the world. The world will still face a time of tribulation, the antichrist, the war of Armageddon, the triumph of Christ, and then a thousand years of His reign. There are also variations on when the rapture will occur, possibly during or even after the time of tribulation. Those who hold a postmillennial view believe that Christian influence will eventually bring light to every part of the earth and then Jesus will return as a triumphant King to an awaiting world of believers. Amillennialists believe that, when Jesus returns, it is all over—no rapture, no tribulation, no thousand years. Heaven begins for those who belong to Christ and hell begins for those who do not. The fourth view is that of the approximate two-thirds of the current world population who do not profess Christ and do not believe He is coming at all.

The fact is, however, that when the Lord Jesus Christ comes to the earth again, He will do exactly what He has planned. We will see how it fits perfectly into the theology of the Word of God as we adjust our theology or worldview. One thing is for sure, there will be a great change.

I say again, it is interesting that Christ uses the analogy of a thief. Yes, they come unexpectedly—and that may be the main emphasis—but they also steal things. What will Jesus steal when He comes? A clue to that answer is found in Luke 17:34: "I tell you that in that night there will be two men in one bed; the one will be taken and the other left." Perhaps this is a rapture scene!

The main point of all of this for our topic is that this thief, Jesus, will come in the night. By "night," I do not mean the natural night as the world is always half in and half out of the darkness and sunshine. Rather, this night-time is called the third watch. It is a time for Christians to be watching, but it also is a time of great spiritual darkness in the world. In John 9:4-5, Jesus said, "The night is coming when no one can work; As long as I am in the world, I am the light of the world." Because Jesus left the world, it is now in darkness.

The enormity of the spiritual darkness in the world cannot be overemphasized. Secularism, atheism, New Age, cults, paganism, false messiahs, materialism, evolution, humanism, demonic strongholds, the rulers of the darkness of this age, and numerous non-Christian religions hold the majority of the world's population in deception and darkness.

Darkness also battles with light. Even within the fold of Christianity and on its borders there are those who wrestle with spiritual deception or the things of the flesh. Christians are not immune to the temptations of lust, greed, power, or fame. They can be subtly lured into spiritual deception, the occult, mysticism, and false religions. That is why the Bible contains so much exhortation for believers.

Christians, however, have a twofold advantage. First, we know the Savior who overcame all temptation as an example for us. Christians don't deny that they need a Savior. We need Him and the guidance of the Spirit of Truth. To resist the darkness of insincerity, hypocrisy, hardness of heart, or love grown cold, we must always check the oil in our lamps and let them burn for Jesus because we need His light to find the way. Second, we know where to find the answers—in the Bible. We must continually hide God's Word in our hearts.

Paul wrote optimistically in Romans 13:12, "The night is far spent, the day is at hand." He used these words as a metaphor to encourage the people in Rome to cast off the works of darkness, put on the armor of light, and walk in the day, which is possible for Christians because we know the One who gives us light. This is confirmed in Paul's message to the Thessalonians when he was conversing with them about Jesus coming as a thief in the night. He bolstered them up by saying they were not of the darkness but "sons of light and sons of the day," and so they would not be surprised by the Lord's sudden coming (1 Thessalonians 5:4-5).

Now even though individual people can be in a place where their "night is far spent" and can accept the light of Jesus Christ so that they enter the daylight, the world as a whole still spins in the darkest of dark nights. This is the spiritual state and condition of the world in which we find ourselves today. The only lamppost, according to Corinthians 4:4, is the one that shines forth "the light of the gospel of the glory of Christ" which changes people's lives. When a Christian walks into a room full of unbelievers, he brings the inner light of Christ into his conversation with them. Praise God for changed lives. One by one, people are coming to the Lord in places all over the world, but the time of His coming again is drawing near. The thief may come at midnight.

The Midnight Hour

Remember the Y2K scare? As each time zone around the world entered into the year 2000, everyone was focusing on midnight and wondering if all the computers would go haywire. There were prayer vigils, celebrations, and frequent media reports keeping us informed whether society was going to have a meltdown. We survived! There were a few reported glitches I guess, but they were trivial in the light of what we were told might happen. The electric power didn't go off, the economy didn't crash, the computers kept on computing, Jesus didn't come, and the world goes on, as we know, at least for now. Yet, into what time are we entering?

This is the midnight hour of the third watch. It is also the midnight hour of the third day if a day of the Lord is reckoned in a twenty-four hour system. I suppose if one wants to get technical, the midnight hour of a *third-watch* thousand-year period would be much longer than the midnight hour of a *third-day* thousand-year period, as the first would be roughly 333 years compared to the latter of about 42 years.

I am sure that the Lord understood these differences, and possibly Moses and Peter as well. The intent of Moses in Psalm 90:4, Peter in 2 Peter 3:8, and the Lord in His teaching on the second and third watches was to help people rise above their daily and yearly aspect of time in order to consider it more from God's eternal perspective. This they did rather than giving us the exact timing of the Lord's return.

If someone is reading this and thinking that I am leading you to a prediction of the exact day and hour of the Lord's return, rest assured that I am not. Jesus may come in the midnight hour of the third watch or even later in the fourth watch. Yet, as Christians we have a responsibility to try to understand the times in which we live. This is an amazing time in history as we are in the midnight hour of both the third watch and the third day. It has not happened before. It will not happen again. The church has entered a time span of approximately forty-two years that is the overlapping of the midnight hour of both the third watch and the third day.

This is significant because the Bible has a couple of important things to say about the midnight hour. First, it was at this hour that the Lord sent His tenth plague and smote the firstborn of Egypt, thus delivering the Hebrews from Pharaoh (Exodus 12:29). This was about 10 P.M. for us in the ancient Israel time system; more importantly, it was their midnight hour. At that time, Pharaoh sent orders to Moses and Aaron and told them to take the Hebrews and leave. Symbolically, Egypt has always represented the world or the world system to Christians. The Lord will one day come and take His people out of the world. It may be in the midnight hour of the church.

The second significant teaching from Scripture regarding the midnight hour is found in Matthew 25:1-13, the parable of the ten virgins. They all went out to meet the bridegroom. The five wise virgins took enough oil for their lamps, but the five foolish virgins did not. They fell asleep and were suddenly awakened by a voice saying that the bridegroom was coming. Guess what time it was? That's right, it was midnight. While the five foolish virgins scampered about trying to locate oil for their lamps, the five wise virgins entered into the wedding with the bridegroom, and the door was shut leaving the five foolish virgins outside. They knocked but the door wouldn't open. The Lord heard them but said that He did not know them.

This parable has been looked at from various perspectives and applied to 1) an individual, 2) the church and the world, or 3) professing Christians. With respect to the individual, each life comes to an end and is judged as to whether the individual's work was fueled by a passion for Christ. Concerning the church and the world, there are many who do good works, but those without the oil of salvation that comes by faith and grace will run dry. And with respect to professing Christians, the wise virgins represent sincere Christians, while the foolish profess Christ but are hypocrites in their hearts. The lamps characterize our outward life, and the oil that of the inward. It is the oil of the Holy Spirit in our lives and it is the grace of God for salvation. As with the parable of the solid foundation found in Matthew 7:24-27, the wise hear the words of the Lord and build upon solid-rock principles, while the foolish disregard the truth and build on the sand.

As Christians, we need to always check our oil gauge, desire more of the Holy Spirit, lean more on His guidance, long for His presence, confess and repent from any sin, and seek purity with Christ. We must be "children of God without fault in the midst of a crooked and perverse generation, among whom you shine as lights in the world" (Philippians 2:15).

Jesus ended the parable of the ten virgins by saying, "Watch therefore, for you know neither the day nor the hour in which the Son of Man is coming" (Matthew 25:13). He has called all Christians to be watchers. This brings us to Part Two in which we will investigate the responsibilities of the servants of the third watch.

QUESTIONS: FOR STUDY, REVIEW AND DISCUSSION

1. Which verses by Paul, Peter, and John speak about the thief in the night? To what do the verses written by Paul and Peter compare the thief in the night? To whom do the verses written by John compare the thief? What will this thief steal?

2. When does this thief come? What Scriptures show that we are in the nighttime of the world?

3. The spiritual darkness in the word is demonstrated in various ways. What are some that the chapter names? What are some that you have seen personally?

4. How is it that we, as Christians, can walk in the light of day in a world full of spiritual darkness? What is our lamppost?

5. To what unique spiritual hour has the church finally arrived? What is the significance of this? What various interpretations are there to the parable of the ten virgins? Which do you believe?

PART TWO

THE SERVANTS OF THE THIRD WATCH

THE HEART OF THE WATCHING SERVANTS

Dr. Cedric Chau and his wife Ivy watch for the Lord from Dublin, Ireland. Cedric's parents sent him from his home in Hong Kong to boarding school in Europe when he was a teenager. He now holds a doctorate degree in business and teaches at one of the universities in Dublin. During his college days, he joined a Bible study for Chinese students. Eventually, the group became a church that Cedric now pastors. Formally known as the Chinese Gospel Church of Dublin, it reaches out to the tens of thousands of Chinese immigrants and refugees dispersed throughout Ireland. Sunday services also draw some of Irish or other European ancestry. Chinese churches throughout Europe invite Pastor Cedric to preach. The Chaus strongly believe in the interconnection between all parts of the global church. Their Dublin church equips its members to be lights in a dark place, to share the Good News, and to gather the harvest before the coming of the Lord.

The Global Church

Have you done much traveling lately? Ever felt a little bit cranky because your 3,000-mile flight was delayed an hour or so, and it messed up your tight schedule of meetings and events? Modern technological advancements give us more opportunity, but I wonder if it has increased our patience.

The world appears much smaller since the birth of the church almost 2,000 years ago. Daniel's prophecy regarding an increase in end-time travel and knowledge (12:4) seems to have been fulfilled in our days. What once were distant undiscovered continents for the ancient mode of travel are now well-known land masses with many populated countries easily reached in a short time by jet. Some say that the amount of knowledge accrued through scientific investigation is doubling every two years. The advancements today would baffle the first century church.

Peter, one of the apostles who witnessed the outpouring of the Holy Spirit on the day of Pentecost and then preached to thousands gathered from many nations (Acts 2), would be absolutely amazed by the growth and impact of the church in the last two millennia. The passion of Christian evangelists and missionaries over the centuries has taken the gospel message of the risen Savior to every corner of the earth. Today, new technology makes communication of biblical truth available to masses of people despite their geographic or political isolation. It has been estimated that one-third of the earth's peoples have been influenced by Christianity, and that one out of every ten persons is a Bible-believing, born-again Christian. Praise God!

The wonderful power of the Holy Spirit is constantly at work, penetrating the stoniest of hearts, healing shattered lives, and transforming societies. His residence in the heart of true believers continually breaks down the traditional barriers of race, ethnic origin, social class, and even denominationalism, and causes a working together in the harvest fields of the world.

The last few years have brought some foreign travel into my ministry and I have been able to see some of the awesome things the Lord is doing around the world as He works interculturally to bring the truths of the Bible to the many different people groups. There are Caucasians smuggling Bibles into China, South Americans taking the Word of God to Israel and Arabia, Africans coming to the United States, and Filipinos going to Asia in service to the Lord. When our mission team was on the streets of Hong Kong, we met a group of Christians from Nigeria doing as we were—evangelizing.

On another occasion, I was in Ireland with Pastor Chau teaching a predominately Chinese Christian church about the danger of cults. We were on the Irish Sea at a retreat center and my English message was being translated into Mandarin and Cantonese.

What led up to the invitation is relevant here! Years ago, a dear couple, Ken and Carmen Martin, had been doing missionary work for years in Ireland, along with their children. Ministry sometimes wounds people and this happened to them. They felt led by the Lord to go back to the United States for healing and new direction, and happened to end up in Idaho in our church. God touched their lives and healing occurred. They became very involved in the church, then suddenly they were called to go back to Ireland by a man they had known and respected there. Thus, our churches became connected. God is awesome, and He is doing things like this all over the world! Another precious couple went from our church south to the border of Texas and Mexico to run a children's home. This brought a connection between our church and a great group of Mexican believers living on the border.

The many different people from distinct cultures crossing over into other cultures is not just an accident. It is a part of God's plan, a component of His ultimate goal which is not just about evangelism and salvation, but about discipleship. The mandate from Jesus was to "Go . . . and make disciples of all nations" (Matthew 28:19). A disciple is one who is disciplined in the ways of the Lord, and Jesus was commanding His followers to disciple all the nations of the world. In other words, He was looking for discipleship of global proportions. His church encompasses those from all nations who have made Him Lord of their lives.

The New Testament word for "church" comes from the Greek word *ekklesia* that literally means "a calling out." For Christians this can apply to either the entire company of the redeemed (Jesus said, "I will build my church"— Matthew 16:18) or to a local assembly of professed believers (1 Corinthians 1:2).

A Servant Is Called to Serve

The global body of believers is penetrating into a new significant time in God's schedule. The entrance into the third watch signifies the need for His church to better discern what attitude the Lord desires of His people during this duration. Let's consider once again the parable of the watching servants.

> Let your waist be girded and your lamps burning; and you yourselves be like men who wait for their *master,* when he will return from the wedding, that when he comes and knocks they may open to him immediately. Blessed are *those servants* whom the *master,* when he comes, will find watching. Assuredly, I say to you that he

will gird himself and have them sit down to eat,
and will come and serve them. And if he should
come in the second watch, or come in the third
watch, and find them so, blessed are *those servants*"

LUKE 12:35-38, EMPHASIS ADDED

It may seem obvious, but it must be stated that the role,
the occupation, the business, or—can I say—the calling of
these individuals in the parable is that of servants whose
role it is to serve. The servants of a master have the sole
purpose of serving that master. Those who call Jesus *Master* are called to serve Him. This is our role, our function,
and our desire. We should diligently search our heart and
ask Him to change anything that makes us an unfit servant.

The Greek word *doulos* is translated "servant," a word
signifying relationship and meaning "slave" or
"bondservant" of a master. In this passage, Jesus is the
Master and we are the bondservants. This is not what we
do; it is who we *are*. Another Greek word signifying the
function of a servant is *diakonos* which denotes the service
of one who is an attendant of the master (i.e., runs errands,
waits upon tables, or does other menial jobs). From this
word, we get the New Testament concept of deacons. In
these words *doulos* and *diakonos*, we see the relationship
and function behind the word "servant."

A simple perusal of the word "servant" in a Bible con-
cordance shows that many people were called servants of
the Lord, including such Old Testament names as Moses,
Samuel, David, Job, Elijah, and even Jonah. In the New
Testament, Jesus referred to His disciples as servants. Some
of the epistles of Paul, as well as those of Peter, James, and
Jude, begin with a proclamation of being a servant of Jesus

Christ. John, Timothy, and Epraphras are called servants of the Lord, and Phoebe is called a servant of the church at Cenchrea (Romans 16:1).

We, as Christians, are not called to be masters but servants of the Lord. This might shock some Christians, as they think they are to overcome every obstacle and master everything in their life through victorious living. There is certainly a measure of truth to that, but we must remember in all of it that we do not become greater than our Master Jesus. It is He whom we serve daily, weekly, monthly, and yearly.

The concept of Christians serving the Lord is strongly implied throughout the New Testament. Even if people are under subjection to an earthly master, when they follow the call to become Christians, their first allegiance is to Jesus Christ. As the apostle Paul implies, "For he that is called in the Lord, being a servant, is the Lord's freeman: likewise also he that is called, being free, is Christ's servant" (1 Corinthians 7:22, KJV).

Paul also lists various attributes that the servant of the Lord should seek to develop within his or her character. Some of these are listed in 2 Timothy 2:24-25 and include gentleness, ability to teach, patience, and humility.

A Servant's Need for Humility and Faithfulness

The trait of humility is at the heart of being a servant. A servant is subject to the master's will and, in a sense, owns nothing and does nothing outside the spectrum of that will. This station of life calls for a heart that is humble because the master calls his servant to obedience and faithfulness and, at a moment's notice, may call him to do something quite contrary to what the servant would choose on his own.

Anyone called to be a servant of God is to be about his heavenly Father's kingdom business. Sometimes that business might put an individual in the limelight of people's focus where he would rather not be. But, most of the time, the kingdom business is done behind the scenes, often immersed in humble, even menial, activity. When the Master calls you to speak a word to someone, send a letter, or visit a neighbor, you are the servant. Your place is not to say, "I don't feel like it. Could you get someone else? I have more important things to do."

The Lord Jesus gave us an illustration of a humble servant in John 13 when He washed the disciples' feet. Just prior to this, He prepared Himself by removing His extra garments (most likely His gown or upper coat) and girding (tying) a towel around His waist. Then He took on the role of the most ignoble attendant and cleaned the dirt off the smelly feet of His disciples.

Jesus had a lot to say about the subject of servants and of service, which could fill several chapters. But for our purpose, it is enough to say that throughout His parables and teachings regarding the role and attitude of servants, there is an emphasis on humility. For example, when His disciples inquired who would be the greatest in the kingdom of heaven, He responded, "Whoever humbles himself as this little child is the greatest in the kingdom of heaven" (Matthew 18:4). In another place when He was stopping a quarrel among the disciples about who would be greatest, He answered and said, "You know that the rulers of the Gentiles lord it over them, and those who are great exercise authority over them. Yet it shall not be so among you; but whoever desires to become great among you, let him be your servant" (Matthew 20:25-26).

Jesus also emphasized a servant's need for faithfulness to the tasks that His master assigned. In one teaching He said, "He who is faithful in what is least is faithful also in much" (Luke 16:10). One who is truly humble will be faithful in whatever the master assigns because there is no hidden agenda or impure motive to do anything but what His master bids. The smallness or greatness of the task is not the issue. Rather, the issue is simply that the master asked it to be done.

Those with a humble attitude will not boast, "Oh, that is beneath my dignity." One who has never washed another's feet, nor done menial labor in the church in order to uphold someone else's ministry, is not yet fit to lead. How can anyone lead unless he or she has learned to follow? How can anyone be of value leading if he or she does not understand the heart of those they lead? And what better place is there to learn this than in the accomplishment of small tasks that show our faithfulness to the Lord.

As servants of the Most High God, Christians are privileged to be used in the kingdom of God wherever and however He bids. Yet sometimes the flesh nature emerges and wars for unhealthy recognition.

It may be that the Lord has called you to into a position of leadership in the kingdom because you were faithful in what was least, and now He has increased you. However, the attitude of the true servant of the Lord is to not only serve Him but to serve those who follow Him as well. So regardless of where the Master has placed us or what He has us doing, we should humbly submit to Him and be of the best service possible to others around us.

The Priority of Character over Gifts

Which do you think is more important, character or giftedness? Some people say "character" but they act as though "giftedness" is more important. Others say the two should be in balance. However, Christian character needs to be prioritized above giftedness. Gifts and talents are important, but they should never be the first priority.

As a pastor in an active church, I have become a little wary of visitors who appear to be church shopping for a place that will allow them to do public ministry without first demonstrating the heart of a servant. Of course, I want people to get involved in the ministry of the local church, and they need to, but there is plenty of work to do behind the scenes. There was a time in our church's history that membership was recognized when a person's name appeared on the nursery schedule. Today, we have to be more cautious than that, but we still maintain that true membership belongs to those who serve the local church in some capacity.

The apostle Paul warned Timothy not to lay hands on anyone quickly (see 1 Timothy 5:22), meaning that Timothy should be careful about placing someone in a Christian leadership role too soon. Sometimes pastors or church leaders might need someone's gift so much that they forget the need to appraise the individual's character before thrusting him in front of the congregation because he has a nice singing voice, communication skills, financial expertise, prophetic insights, or the faith to heal.

With regard to traveling ministers, I want to know who do they look to as their pastor? Are they accountable to someone? Do they belong to a denomination or ministerial association that provides a true covering or are they acting like a hotshot, a lone ranger who is above all of that? What are their views of local church and its leadership? If I invite them to speak, do they see themselves as being under or over the authority of the elders in that local church? If they are prophetic, are they truly bringing a word from the Lord for the congregation, or are they simply trying to fill their schedule and pay the bills?

Certainly, there are many gifted people in the kingdom of God today. However, their gifts must be balanced with godly character. The Lord examines our hearts to know our motives. If our motives are sincere, then the sharing of our gifts and talents will be acceptable before Him. In fact, He will create opportunities for us to use them and thus grow in ability. But if we become prideful, then even He will resist us because "God resists the proud, but gives grace to the humble" (1 Peter 5:5).

God looks for people with humble attitudes to serve Him in His kingdom and make ready for His return. As 1 Corinthians 1:26-29 states, God does not normally call the wise, mighty, or noble; but He calls those who, in the world's eyes, appear foolish, weak, base, and despised so that no flesh should glory in His presence.

The Heart of a Servant

What should be in the heart of a servant ? Well, as we have seen, a servant should understand the position of service. It is an honor to serve the Master Jesus. We are not the masters; we are the servants. Jesus is the Master. Each of us should seek for hearts of humility and to be faithful servants who do the bidding of our Lord, no matter how trivial it may seem. This is our occupation. This is our employment. We may have jobs where we work and make money to provide for families, but in our hearts we must first be servants of the Lord. This is our humble office and station in life. When we have the sincere heart of a servant of the Lord, then we can perform the tasks that our Master requires in a manner that will please Him.

What is your role in service to the Master? Although a question like this may be difficult to fully answer, one who serves the Lord should be able to name a few specific things. How do you serve in your local church? Whom do you pray for? What people have heard you share your testimony? What money have you given to missions or mercy ministries? How often do you draw near to Jesus and ask Him if He has a task for you? Are you being faithful in the little things God has called you to do?

It can't be overemphasized in this day, when people's character demonstrates high levels of independence and rebellion to authority, that the main role of the servant is to serve. Jesus is the Master and we are the servants. Our heart should be open to Him and soft to His ways. When it gets hard or calloused, we need to let the oil of the Holy Spirit soften it. Sometimes people spend years running from the Master's call and, in so doing, they get caught up in activities that do not edify them. When people want to be master of their own lives, do what they want to do, and go where they want to go, they often run up against a brick wall. Then they justify their actions by blaming their troubles on others,. Eventually, they may realize their need to submit to the Master and His plans for their lives. Christians are called to lay down their kingship and get off the throne. They are called to be servants and have hearts as servants of the Lord.

The watching servants were assigned several tasks of preparation in readiness for Christ's return. The role of the global church should be the same.

QUESTIONS: FOR STUDY, REVIEW AND DISCUSSION

1. How is the prophecy in Daniel 12:4 regarding an increase in end-time travel and knowledge being fulfilled in our days?

2. Consider the Greek words *doulos* and *diakonos*. What do they mean and how do they apply to a Christian's relationship and function in the church? What basic things should servants do? Who are we to serve? Have you ever tried to be the master and not the servant? Explain.

3. Discuss why humility and faithfulness are so important for servants. What examples of the servant do we learn from Jesus' teachings and life? Read 2 Timothy 2:24-25 and make a list of the various characteristics that Paul mentions about servants.

4. Should we seek to have a balance between godly character and talents? Why or why not? Have you ever met Christians who were talented but lacked the character necessary to fill a position of responsibility? Have you ever been drawn to talent over godly character? Why is

God more concerned about your character than your talents? Are talents and gifts also important?

5. What heart of service should Christians have with respect to their Master Jesus?

THE TASKS OF THE WATCHING SERVANTS

Linda Sisson watches for the Lord from Dallas, Texas. After years of teaching the deaf, she felt the call to go to Christ for the Nations to become equipped for mission work. For over seven years she worked as a children's evangelist in Latin America and as a teacher of praise and worship, coming alongside pastors and helping churches. As a single woman, she was able to give herself to that chore fully, and many lives were touched by her compassion and outreach. Eventually, she was released by the Holy Spirit from this task and led back to the States where she accepted a unique social-worker position in which she is able to be a blessing to the poor and share with them the love of Jesus. She would be described as a prayer warrior by any who know her well. By saving her money and taking vacation time, she fulfills other tasks for the Lord by going to places like the Jerusalem prayer house and praying for the Jews to receive Jesus as their Messiah before He comes the second time, or with the reconciliation team that walked through the Muslim country of Turkey asking forgiveness for the wrong deeds done by supposed Christians to the Muslims during the Crusades.

The Master Entrusting His Servants

Have you ever thought about how much confidence and trust the Lord has indicated He has in His servants by leaving the world in their hands until He returns?

It is a scary thought! In a small way, it might be compared to parents who leave their kids for a while and give them a list of chores to do. Perhaps it is vacuuming, doing the dishes, cleaning their bedroom, or watching a little brother or sister. Always, however, the implied intent—even if not stated—is, "Stay out of trouble."

One time my parents told my thirteen-year-old brother, Terry, to watch my sister who was eight, and me, a scrawny five-year-old. Mom and Dad finally got a chance to go out by themselves and they took it. They were great parents to us and they deserved a night out.

This is actually the only time I remember my brother being in charge of us. Perhaps the events of the night led to his demise in that leadership role. You see there was an accident. I say *accident* because we didn't mean for it to happen. Yet, it certainly was our fault because it could have been avoided if we hadn't been messing around. Or maybe I should say *I* instead of *we* since I was the one trying to run down my brother and sister with my pedal-powered go-cart. However, they didn't seem to mind as they were gleefully hopping to and fro on pogo sticks on our concrete basement floor.

That's when my sister Rodeen's pogo stick had a problem. The metal worked its way through the rubber boot as she jumped out of the way of my go-cart. When the metal hit the floor, it skidded and, with a slam, she went face first on the concrete. She lay there while I kept trying to run down Terry and we both said, "Come on, Rodeen, get up and play."

When we saw the blood, we realized something bad had happened and the game was over. One of her front teeth was lying on the floor and another one was bent. While my brother frantically phoned everywhere he could to get hold of my parents, I was to stand watch over my sister who now was perched with her mouth under the bathroom sink faucet. Being only five, I wasn't quite aware of the fact that she had passed out in the sink which was filling with water. When I realized that her head was below the water and she wasn't moving, I yelled for my brother who came and pulled her out of the sink. Thankfully, my parents were located and my sister taken to the hospital. If we couldn't have located them, they would have come home unprepared for what had happened.

When the Lord returns, what will He find? Will He find servants who have humbly and faithfully kept His house in good shape and ready for His return, or will He find accidents, chaos, lack of preparation, and the chores not done? How will His children be getting along?

Leaders Should Be Servants

The parable of the watching servants focuses more on the role of Christian leaders as the servants of Christ and His people than it does on lay people. However, the parable is certainly applicable to all Christians because all are called to be ministers of Christ and all will give an account, thereby sharing the blessings when He returns.

Within a large house with many servants, some of those servants are called to lead, or be in charge of, other servants. They are to serve the Master by serving in positions of authority, and one aspect of this would be to serve the other servants. As Jesus said, "If anyone desires to be first, he shall be the last of all and servant of all" (Mark 9:35). This is the basic law of God's kingdom. If you want to be in charge, you must learn to serve. If you want to be a leader, you must first learn to be a follower.

Learning to serve the Lord and His people is not easy. Learning to follow the leadership of the Holy Spirit and lead His people is not easy. Learning to work in harmony with the other servant-leaders in the house is not easy. Yet, those who would serve as leaders require an attitude that will embrace these things.

As we consider the tasks of the watching servants in the parable, we need to realize that they apply to *all* Christians as servants, but most definitely must be employed by the servant-leaders in the church today.

Tasks of the Servants

Fortunately for us, the assignments of the Lord are not burdensome. They actually are a part of the preparation process whereby those servants who employ them will be making ready for His return. Moreover, the completion of the tasks is essentially a major portion of the watch duty. Like the parent who assigns the oldest child to watch over the youngest one, there is an aspect in the fulfillment of that responsibility that is the *watch*.

The servants in the parable (Luke 12:35-38) were asked to do several things in preparation for their master's return. An important key for us to understand regarding these chores is that the fulfillment of them helps define for us the basics of what it means to watch. The four duties of the servants were that they should have their waists girded, their lamps burning, wait for their master, and open the door when he knocks.

If you have ever wondered what the Lord is going to expect from you on His return, or wondered what your responsibilities are on your watch, then pay close attention as we consider the following tasks of Christians. The fulfillment of these tasks shows what the Lord means when He uses the word *watch*. Let's look again at the portion of the parable that reveals the tasks, and then briefly investigate each of these concepts.

> *Let your waist be girded* and *your lamps burning;* and you yourselves *be like men who wait for their master,* when he will return from the wedding, *that when he comes and knocks they may open to him immediately.* Blessed are those servants whom the master, when he comes, will find watching
> LUKE 12:35-37, EMPHASIS ADDED

First Task: The Servants Were to Have Their Waist Girded

At that point in history, people often wore long robes called tunics. The tunics in Palestine were probably knee length or longer, and were made by sewing together two pieces of cloth—wool or linen—leaving a hole for the head and neck. It was worn with a belt around the waist, and the sleeves normally extended to at least the elbows.

Servants often tucked their long robes into their belts to be better able to move about freely and energetically. The expression "gird up your loins" is used in various places in Scripture to suggest the idea of tucking the tunic into the belt for flexibility in service. The idea of girding here speaks of two things: preparation for service, and the actual act of service.

This first area of preparation for service is a vital part of Christian readiness. This does not just highlight the idea of readiness for the Lord's return, but for living *this* life as a mature and truthful Christian. The apostle Peter exhorts Christians to "gird up the loins of your mind" (1 Peter 1:13). It's too easy to let our robe hang down, get in the lounging mode, say that someone else can do the chores, and forget that we are called to live the Christian life.

Preparation for service in God's kingdom requires a certain level of training and changing. When one is born into the kingdom of God, regardless of his natural age, there are certain stages of spiritual growth that must occur before maturity is attained. The Father dearly loves newborns, but He knows they aren't capable of girding up their loins for service. This takes growth and discipline in discipleship.

A part of the means by which growing will occur is by the digestion of the Word of God. The Bible is aptly referred to as "the pure milk" (1 Peter 2:2) for new converts and "solid food" (Hebrews 5:12) for mature Christians. Feeding upon Scripture should be a daily diet for the children of God. This, however, is only one substance necessary for growth and discipline. Quality time in prayer and meditation to Jesus, the "bread of life" (John 6:35), is another. There are also experiences that come through taking steps of faith. God will literally put His children through tests to see what they have learned. Have you had tests of your faith lately? This is the hand of your heavenly Father maturing you.

The Holy Spirit, whose job it is to guide God's children into all truth, will use all means necessary to grow, train, and bring change to those called to be servants of the most high God. Truth and truthfulness are a big issue with God. Those who are called to serve are to do so in the utmost honesty and integrity of heart. Paul wrote to the Ephesians that they should have their waists girded with truth. This, he says, is one of the ways by which Christians can stand against all the wiles of the devil and the evil of the day (Ephesians 6:10-14).

The idea, then, of preparation for service, is the process through which the trainee must be taken by the trainer to that point in which he is fully developed and schooled. The trainee now is of age and understands his position as servant. He has gathered up any hindering garments that might adversely affect his walk or ability to freely move about, and is ready to engage in acts of service with the highest level of truthfulness and integrity.

The second area of this task implies actual service. The reason for preparation is an outcome of quality service. A woman who makes great preparation for serving guests an elegant dinner will not have actually accomplished the goal until everyone has dined with delight. The preparation of the dinner on the woman's part, however, is in itself an act of service to the guests prior to them dining. So it is with Christians. In the process of discipleship and learning to gird up our loins, there is work being done to prepare for the Master's return. The phase of learning to be a servant of the Lord is, in fact, service to Him because we are doing it as a result of His impact upon our lives and His desire for us to serve Him.

Preparation for each servant will be similar because all are called to serve with the appropriate attitude and understanding, but there will also be some differences. This is because each servant is unique and will be given responsibilities in accordance with individual talents or kingdom needs.

Christians need to increase their attitude of readiness today for the Lord's return by heeding the call to be servants. How does this apply to daily pragmatic Christian living? A part of the answer can be found in the modern-day equivalent of "gird up your loins," which simply means to "roll up your sleeves and get to work." People who are constantly looking for the big picture of God's will for their lives often miss out on the little opportunities for service right in front of them.

Have you ever noticed how many young people today seem confused about God's will for their lives? Some of them think that they need their whole future revealed before they can take any step of action. Well, it normally doesn't work that way. When they ask me for advice, I often tell them the first thing to do is to pray and ask God to reveal the first step. It is amazing how many times we neglect this simple step. Then I tell them to consider the possibilities and step out in the one they most feel has God's favor. Finally, I tell them that God knows their heart and that they are trying to please Him. He will help them find His will and take it one step at a time.

Second Task: The Servants Were to Have Their Lamps Burning

The lamps were open vessels of clay, bronze, or gold filled with oil and a floating wick, and they were set in strategic places to give the most light. At the time Jesus taught this parable in ancient Palestine, the lamps were often small, short, somewhat round containers that could fit into the palm of the hand. They normally had a hole in the center into which the oil was poured, and another smaller hole near the edge for the wick. It was the servants' responsibility to replenish the oil and trim the wicks.

The lamp speaks to us of the Word of God. Psalm 119:105 says, "Your word is a lamp to my feet and a light to my path." We need to let the light of God's Word shine before us so that we can know where to go, and we need the light of the Word's character to shine through our lives for others to see. Our character should be such that it helps others see the truth, and the words of the Bible should so impact us that others see Jesus in us. It is our responsibility to hold out the Bible proudly as we proclaim its life-changing truth and attributes. The light of the glorious gospel of truth, held within the lives of the servants of the Lord, suffuses the darkest hearts and opens the eyes of those who would come to God.

During my years of searching for truth, someone impacted me with the light of Christ. I was working at a Montgomery Ward's warehouse in Reno, Nevada, in the summer of 1973. My mind was totally fried from drugs, philosophy and eastern religion books, and numerous occult activities. I was striving to escape from this world which I had come to believe did not really exist except in my mind. I was really messed up. God knew that I needed someone so He brought Tad into my life. Bold, and yet gentle, he would sit next to me at break and lunch and open his Bible.

I was introverted in those days, and I talked to no one unless forced to, but Tad wouldn't leave me alone. He would pester me until I read aloud from his Bible the words in John 8:12 in which Jesus said, "I am the light of the world." That was all I had to read, but then he would repeat it and explain it to me. Every day he would do this, sometimes more than once. One day, he yelled at me from the other end of the warehouse, "I'M TELLING YOU, STAN, JESUS

IS THE LIGHT OF THE WORLD!" People were looking at him, then at me, then at him. It was incredible.

This was pretty difficult for me to take. The next day, after only a couple of weeks of it, I quit. But those words would not leave me alone. They were present when I would astral project or when I walked through a wilderness region or when I stared at the sun. God used those words and that message to help me see the truth of His ways and His life for me. He healed my mind and gave me new life in Him. It didn't happen immediately as I was in great deception, but He gave me His light and eventually I was set free! All you who know Jesus have your own testimony of His coming into your life and giving you His light. There are many more who need this light and there is a lot of work to do to spread the truth about Jesus Christ. The servants of the house may have different talents and abilities, some small and some great, but the work is great enough that it requires each one to get involved in the area of his gifting. How often do church leaders plead for someone to teach Sunday school classes, or start an adult Bible study discipleship group, or be a part of mercy ministry outreaches, or go on short-term missions? And how many respond to the call?

The opportunities to serve are beyond counting. Jesus said, "The harvest is truly great, but the laborers are few" (Luke 10:2). Not only are there innumerable opportunities for service, but the methods for serving are endless, as well. I heard a story about a woman who witnessed in public restrooms. She would go into one stall and remove all the toilet paper, then she would wait in the next stall until someone occupied the stall with no paper and was in need. She would courteously offer paper to the distressed individual, a little at a time. While dispersing the paper, the Christian woman talked about the glories of the Lord and witnessed up a storm to the toilet-paper-deprived-individual. I know this sounds funny, but she actually led quite a few people to the Lord in this manner. Hey, if I can have someone yelling at me from across a warehouse about Jesus being the Light of the World, anything is possible.

Spreading the light of Jesus is what is important. The Holy Spirit says to this one, "Call and encourage Sister-So-and-So," or to that one He says, "Don't forget to send a Christian birthday card to your dad," or He might lead us to pray at a moment's notice for someone, or do a host of other things that appear insignificant to us. Yet, He is the Master Planner. He weaves together all of the needs and all of the solutions. Each partner in service is vital and plays a role that helps fulfill the entire plan.

Task Three: The Servants Were to Wait

We can learn some great things about the concept of waiting from these servants in the parable. For instance, they do not appear to be anxious or upset that they had to wait. They just continued to make preparations for his return as servants customarily do. This parable does not specifically say where they were to wait, but it is implied that it was at the master's home, as he would come back after an evening out and knock at the door.

I think we sometimes get the wrong ideas about having to wait for the Lord's return. What are our motives for wanting Him to return? Do we want Him to come so that we can simply escape our daily problems and circumstances, or do we wish to dismiss our responsibility of making preparations or being a light to others? The proper motive for wanting Him to return is our love for Him and our desire to be with Him. There is nothing wrong with a longing in our hearts to be with our Master, but still we must wait.

Here is another point to consider: If we really have entered the third watch, then that means a first and second watch went before us. Noble Christians have been waiting for the Lord's return for 2,000 years. In fact, every generation of Christians who has ever lived believed that the Lord was going to return in their lifetime. But we are still here and Jesus hasn't returned yet because there is more preparation and more service to be done before that time.

A certain dynamic occurs between waiting and watching. The word *watch* is a key to the whole parable. It concerns our attitude and gives us the idea of remaining awake and being vigilant. We need to keep our eyes on the door because the Lord could return at any moment. At the same time, we are to wait patiently and finish the work He has given us to do.

There is a sense of tension for Christians between the task of waiting and the overall notion of watching. However, God knows that this internal pressure is good for us and keeps us in balance. If we focus too much on the wonders that will occur when Jesus comes, then we take our eyes off the job that is still to be done. On the contrary, if we focus too little on the Lord's return, it is easy to lose heart for the task at hand. We are to wait patiently and do the job that God has called us to, and at the same time we are to watch and eagerly anticipate His return.

Someone once said, "Christians should live as though Jesus is returning today but plan out their lives as though He will not return for a thousand years." This is wise counsel. Parents should not neglect to plan for their children or grandchildren's future because they rationalize that Jesus will come today. Many have done this and lived to regret it.

Sadly, there are stories of people who have determined to not buy a home, go to college, pursue a career, save for retirement, get married or have children because they thought that the world would end on a certain day or time. When they realized that their prime productive years were over and Jesus had not yet come, they sometimes blamed a certain teaching, a pastor who taught it, or even the Lord. But they are the ones who have lost out.

My point is this: Even though we hope and might believe that Jesus will come in our lifetime, we must employ the principles of Scripture when it comes to our lives and families. We wait and we watch. Both the waiting and watching are done in practical ways. We will investigate this more in the next chapter.

Task Four: The Servants Were to Open Immediately to the Master's Knock

Notice the anticipation with which the servants were waiting. The clue is in the phrase, "when he comes and knocks they may open to him immediately." Wherever the servants were located in the house, they were listening for the master's knock. Listening and being ready are keys to this task.

How can we listen and be ready for our Master's knock? Well, in order to listen for His voice, we must first know His voice. John 10:3-4 says, "To Him the doorkeeper opens and the sheep hear His voice . . . for they know His voice." Christians learn to know the voice of the Lord beginning at their first encounter with Him. Christ says in Revelation, "Behold, I stand at the door and knock. If anyone hears My voice and opens the door, I will come in to him and dine with him, and he with Me" (3:20). In a great sense, then,

Christians have already opened the door of their hearts to Jesus.

According to John 14:23, both Jesus and God the Father make their "home" with those who love God and keep His Word. Furthermore, Galatians 4:6-7 tells us that each one of us has the "Spirit" of Jesus, the Son, in our hearts so that we are no longer "a slave but a son," serving our Master Jesus. A son knows his father's voice; a son also knows the voice of the master of the house.

Now, even though Christians have opened their spiritual lives to Jesus, thus attaining salvation, there will come the day when the resurrected Lord will return and the door to our lives will be opened eternally.

It should be noted that the above verse from Revelation was spoken by the Lord in way of admonition to the Laodicean church because they were lukewarm. Some think that this church symbolizes the spiritual condition of the church in the earth today—the last days' church. Others think it represents only a part of the church, or a spiritual, backslidden condition that one may fall into if not careful. However, the servants in the parable of the watching servants have no *if* in their listening and readiness for the Lord's knock at the door. They will open the door *immediately* as they are ready and waiting for the Master. These servants are very watchful.

The four tasks listed above help us to actually define the basics of what it means to watch. The servants' waists girded, the lamps burning, the waiting, and the opening of the door give us some parameters to consider as we try to serve the Lord. But there is another angle to watching that must be considered. This aspect might prove to be even more difficult than those listed above because it requires a persistent patience of watching God to see what He has done, is doing, and will do.

QUESTIONS: FOR STUDY, REVIEW AND DISCUSSION

1. Why must those who lead first learn to follow? Why must Christian leaders know how to serve others? Imagine what it would be like to be one of the servants in the parable of the watching servants. What would your attitude be?

2. Consider the first task of the servants. What does the traditional concept of girding your waist mean? How does this apply to us today? For instance, when you ponder on your own thought processes, what does "gird up the loins of your mind" mean to you? How can preparation for service actually be a part of service itself?

3. Consider the second task of the servants. Describe the lamps that the parable refers to. What do they represent in our lives today? What is your testimony? How did you come to know the light of Jesus? Share it with others.

4. Consider the third task of the servants. Search your heart. What is your reason for wanting the Lord to return? If it is true that every generation of Christians has thought the Lord would return in their lifetime, then what implications does this have for us today? What dynamic tension exists between the concepts of watching and waiting?

5. Consider the fourth task of the servants. Where do you think the servants would be positioned in relationship to the door? What does the door represent to us? Do you know the voice of the Shepherd? Discuss the voice of the Lord with others. How does the Spirit of God speak to you?

THE WATCHFULNESS OF THE WATCHING SERVANTS

Herman and Betsy Bouwhuizen watch for the Lord from Delft, Holland. Herman was born in Holland but moved to the United States when he was a boy. After growing up, he ran a computer business for about twenty years. Several years ago, he and his wife, Betsy, became convinced that the Lord was calling them to become missionaries to Holland so they got out of the computer business, made the arrangements, and headed to Holland to be a support ministry in a church in Delft. From this location, they are able to minister within the local church, to the community, and throughout Holland and Europe. The Bouwhuizens run cell groups and an adult Bible school, teach marriage seminars, host visiting ministries, take prayer teams to Antwerp, Belgium, go on mission trips, and try to bring unity to ministries within Delft. Betsy plays guitar and leads worship in the church and at various ministry conferences. The Lord transplanted them from the United States into Holland and gave them a burden of intercessory prayer for Europe. They watch to see what the Lord is doing in Holland and Europe.

An Emphasis on Watching

People use their eyes constantly but that does not mean they are really observant and watching. It is one thing to quickly glance at something and then turn away; it is quite another to carefully observe something over a period of time and contemplate. Watching can be a pleasant experience such as observing ducks on a lake on a nice summer day. However, it can also be a necessary duty as for the watchman in the tower. Motives for watching might be noble or they might be devious. Looking out for a less fortunate individual is noble, but stalking someone for malicious reasons is criminal and can lead to prosecution.

When the devil or his demons watch people, it is certainly with malicious, ulterior motives. His goal is to plot a person's downfall, hoping to bring temptation at just the right time of weakness. Isaiah 29:20 says that "all who watch for iniquity are cut off."

As Christians, we don't normally consider the believer's call to watch, but in many places in the Bible the followers of God were asked to do just that. Sometimes the important thing was to watch simply to see what the Lord would do. There is much for us to learn from these biblical examples.

Animal Hotels and Birth Pains

Noah was commissioned to build the ark and bring in the animals, but once this was accomplished he had to watch and see what the Lord would do next. If no waters came, he would have simply built a nice hotel for animals—not a very profitable endeavor. He would have been ridiculed and his faith in God mocked.

Just like Noah, believers are sometimes led by the Spirit to step out in faith in a certain thing and then wait and watch to see what the Lord will do. We might put great effort into a project or ministry in preparation and anticipation. However, there comes a point in time when we have done what we can in our own efforts. Then it is up to the Lord to "rain" upon us from on high, to show that He was the one who called us into the project, and then called us to watch and see what He would do.

If God doesn't get involved, all of our preparations are for nothing. People will wonder if we really heard from the Lord. Eventually, we will even question it. Some may try to cause something to happen in their own strength and say that it is God's involvement. The point is, we come to a place where we can do nothing else but watch for the Lord's outpouring or answer.

Conversely, if the Holy Spirit gives us an assignment, we need to do it in preparation for what the Lord will do at the appropriate time. Noah was instructed to build the ark. If he had insisted that the Lord go first with His plan, what would have happened? How could the floods come before the ark was built? If he had said, "I'm not going to place myself in a position of ridicule before the Lord does His thing," then he would have thwarted God's specific plan of using him. He had to trust in the Lord and what He was saying to him. He had to believe and have confidence that God would not put him in a position of failure.

Today, many are not willing to take a risk for God, even after He has assured them that it will all work out if they will but trust in Him and do what He has asked them to do. They want to see what He is going to do before they take the time to do what He has directed them to do. In other words, they want to put "the cart before the horse." This is not possible. God wants to know our faith level. Hebrews 11 tells us that "it is impossible to please God without faith."

This has application that is both general and specific. In a general sense, He tells us to build something that will protect us and those we love from the storms of life. If we say, "I will wait to see if the storms really come before I build," then we will not be protected when those storms come.

There is also specific application. Someone prays and says, "Lord, I want to own a home." The Lord says, "Start saving your money and watch what I will do for you." However, the individual neglects to save his money and thinks, "That was probably not the Lord speaking to me. He is big enough to give me the home without my saving the money." So he places his faith in the wrong area. God told him to save his money to teach him prudence and patience, but the man had his eyes set only on the goal, rather than the process of attaining the goal. God wanted the man's faith to be built by following a simple plan, but the man wanted to complicate and change it. He tricked himself into thinking that his faith was bigger, supposing that God would simply give him a home. In due time, a home appears that would have been perfect for the man, but he didn't have the money to purchase it or even make a down payment. He would have had the money, but he neglected to follow God's plan and then watch what He would do.

Consider Abraham; he was powerless to create a babe in Sarah's womb. The Lord had a plan, but Abraham and Sarah had to wait for His timing. The perfect plan would not happen in man's time but in the Lord's. All they could do was watch and wait. Sarah couldn't quite accept God's plan, however, so she asked Abraham to take her handmaid, Hagar, and have a child through her. This was man's plan and timing, not God's. The result was the birth of Ishmael. But this was not the only result. Enmity broke out between Sarah and Hagar. It might even be fair to say that confusion was a result.

In Genesis 17:17-18, we see Abraham laughing and questioning what he understood to be the Lord's plan and asking that Sarah's plan, Ishmael, might find the Lord's favor instead. In the next few verses, the Lord gently corrects Abraham and assures him that He will bless Ishmael, but that He will also carry through with His plan of Abraham and Sarah having a child in their old age that they shall name Isaac. It is with Isaac that He will establish His covenant.

We know that the Lord's plan and His timing eventually happened and that Abraham and Sarah had their son, Isaac, at a very old age. Hagar was forced to leave and take Ishmael with her. Eventually, both Ishmael and Isaac had children and from their progeny came two great nations, Arabia from Ishmael and Israel from Isaac. Today, there is still great enmity between these nations.

This is an example of what can happen to us when we step out of God's plan and God's timing into our own. We mess things up and unwittingly create enmity and confusion. We are called to watch, but instead we get involved with our own plan and then ask the Lord to make it His plan. He has His own plan and His is better. I am glad that Abraham is referred to in the Bible as the "friend of God" and that his belief was counted to him for "righteousness." He had to go through spiritual birth pains to learn patience and watch for the Lord's timing.

So many of us make mistakes by doing things in our own way and time. It would be easy for us to become discouraged and give up altogether, but, somehow, the Lord is able to bypass even our mistakes and make things turn out for the best. His plan still gets accomplished. How much better it would be, however, and how much confusion we could save in our lives if we would simply wait for His timing and His plan.

Are We To Ponder or to Act?

The prophet Habakkuk adds another dimension to the concept of watching. He prophesied to the nation of Judah just prior to the Babylonian invasion. Habakkuk questioned why God allowed the violence, strife, and contention to continue unchecked in Judah. God answered the prophet saying, "Look among the nations and watch—Be utterly astonished! For I will work a work in your days which you would not believe, though it were told you" (Habakkuk 1:5). The word *watch* here comes from the Hebrew word *nabat* meaning "to scan" with the idea of looking intently. To me, it sounds like God—in answering the prophet's question—was telling him to slow down a little and ponder what was happening among the nations.

God goes on to explain to Habakkuk that He would use the fierce and violent Chaldeans to bring judgment upon Judah. This answer astonished the prophet, and he inquired why a holy God would use such a wicked people to punish those who were more righteous than they. He then retreats to his place of *watch* (watchtower) to see how God would respond.

God answers by telling Habakkuk to "write the vision" that would be used at an appointed future moment. A part of the vision God gave was a contrast between the proud and the just. The proud were not upright in their soul "but the just shall live by his faith" (Habakkuk 2:4), a statement that would one day spark the Protestant Reformation begun by Martin Luther in 1517 when he received the revelation of salvation through faith rather than dead works. God also informed Habakkuk that the wicked will give an account of their deeds and that the books will be balanced in His time, not ours (Habakkuk 2:4-20).

The book of Habakkuk gives us the picture that it is right to ask God even the difficult questions if we have the right heart attitude. He is not angry with us for it, neither is He afraid to answer, although His answer might astonish us. It might even challenge us to get out of the box of our viewpoint and see things from His perspective. As in this case, He might simply say, "Watch and ponder what I will do." This is all we are required to do. It is a part of our watch.

We see the wickedness of society around us, and because we care enough to bring it to God in prayer, He reveals to us a greater revelation than we previously had. Our watch has been enlarged. Our horizons have expanded because we have conquered tunnel vision. We have grown in our understanding of how God handles things. We have looked out past our narrow perspective and have seen the *watch* from a godly vantage point.

There are other times when action on our part is called for in the watch, as we see in the story of Joash, a descendant of King David (2 Chronicles 23). Athaliah, a wicked woman, had murdered all the other heirs of the house of Judah, thinking she had destroyed them all. She then reigned for six years. But when the right time came, the priest Jehoiada plotted to restore the throne to Joash who had been hidden away safely, in order to turn the people from serving false gods.

It was a Sabbath day. Much of the military was in on the revolt, the Levites positioned in various places keeping watch at the doors, or at the king's house, or at the Gate of the Fountain. The priests and other serving Levites were in the house of the Lord where the king was for the coronation service. Other people were told to stay in the courts of the house of the Lord, but no matter where people were positioned, they were given this charge: "All the people shall keep the watch of the Lord" (2 Corinthians 23:6).

The Hebrew "watch" used here is *mishmereth*, the feminine form of *mishmar*, which gives us the idea of the act or charge to keep watch, rather than a man who was in the watchtower as a guard. As the story unfolds, this watch of the Lord eventually included crowning the king, executing Athaliah and her followers, tearing down the temple of Baal and killing Mattan the priest of Baal, appointing new oversight in the house of the Lord, reestablishing the praise and worship of David's time, setting new people to watch over the gates, and setting the king on his throne.

The watch of the Lord may often mean getting involved in restoring righteousness and standing against wickedness. But, as we learned with Habakkuk, it must be in God's timing and God's way. The important thing here is that there was a single unity among those who desired to see the true king on the throne and righteousness restored. All of God's people worked together against the wickedness surrounding them, and they were victorious. When Christians come together in unity to accomplish something according to God's will or promise, the job gets completed and the enemy is conquered.

We see, then, that *watching to see what the Lord will do* is a concept that has been around for a long time. It would be easy to make a long list of biblical people and see how they had to be patient and watch. Just to consider a few, there is Joseph in an Egyptian prison (Genesis 39–40) watching to see how the Lord would bring about the dreams of his childhood (Genesis 37). There is Moses standing before Pharaoh watching to see how the Lord would deliver Israel (Exodus 7). We see the Hebrew children positioned before the Red Sea (Exodus 14) and watching to see how the Lord would save them from the Egyptian armies. We could consider Ruth who watched what would happen as she obeyed Naomi, and Queen Esther who watched how the Lord would deliver her people from Haman and his wicked plot. There are also the many prophets who prophesied and then watched to see what the Lord would do.

Miracles, Tongues, and Attitudes of Expectancy

Then there are the disciples who could do nothing better than to follow Jesus and watch to see what He would do—a healing here, a feeding there, or walking on water, stopping the storm, raising people from the dead, etc. What could they really do but watch and learn from His example and His teachings? His timing was perfect! His plan was perfect!

The one thing they had to develop was an attitude of expectancy. Every day with Jesus was an adventure of profound teachings, revelations, healings, and other miracles. They had peered with their eyes beyond the natural order of things into the supernatural eyes of the Master, and they were changed. They were constantly wondering what was going to happen next.

At Gethsemane, they could do nothing but stand by and watch as their Lord was betrayed, condemned, and crucified. During the three days after His death, what could they do but watch and wait to see what would happen? After His resurrection, He appeared to them at various times and in various places. Examples of this are His appearance to Mary, to the two men on the way to Emmaus, to the ten disciples, to Thomas and the disciples, at the Sea of Tiberias, and prior to His ascension into heaven (John 20:16; Luke 24:15; Luke 24:36; John 20:26; John 21:1, Acts 1:8). During these forty days, the disciples constantly looked for Jesus, expecting Him to come.

Notice what the Bible says that the people (over 500 according to 1 Corinthians 15:6) were doing at the time of the ascension:

> Now when He had spoken these things, *while they watched*, He was taken up, and a cloud re-

> ceived Him out of their sight. And while they
> looked steadfastly toward heaven as He went up,
> behold, two men stood by them in white apparel,
> who also said, "Men of Galilee, why do you stand
> gazing up into heaven? This same Jesus, who
> was taken up from you into heaven, will so come
> in like manner as you saw Him go into heaven"
> ACTS 1:9-11, EMPHASIS ADDED

I would have been watching also, and I probably would have been standing there mesmerized, expecting something else to happen when the angels showed up. It was one of the most significant events in human history. Everyone that was there was intently watching as Jesus ascended. The two men dressed in white apparel were obviously angels letting the people know that this event was all over. Angels had announced Jesus' birth to shepherds keeping watch over their flocks by night (Luke 2), and now angels were announcing that Jesus' time on earth was over as they stood watching. There was nothing left to see at the moment.

The next step was to follow the directions of Jesus. He had previously spoken to them about going to Jerusalem where they would watchfully wait for the outpouring of the Holy Spirit. Once again, they had to go to a place to wait and watch what the Lord would do. They did this by joining together "with one accord in prayer and supplication" (Acts 1:14). Then it happened! The Spirit was poured out, tongues were given, people were saved, and the New Testament church was given genuine birth (see Acts 2).

The people were not only gathered together in unity, but they were *expecting* something to happen as they watched and waited for the promise of the Lord. The eyes of their hearts were on the Lord. They were in suspense, waiting eagerly for what God would do. Lack of faith was not an issue at this time. In fact, the word faith is not even mentioned with regard to what happened there. They did not have to build up their faith level. They knew God was going to fulfill His promise and they simply watched for Him to show up and do what He would do.

Christians today could learn from this as they ask God to heal someone or seek the baptism of the Holy Spirit with tongues. We need to get our eyes off of ourselves and on the Lord, knowing that He is going to do *something*. It might not be in our way or our thinking or our timing, but we need to tarry for Him, waiting with suspense that He will do something amazing.

I appreciate the fact that the disciples watched Jesus until He was out of sight, but then went on to do what they were instructed. If they had just stood in the place where Jesus ascended and had been mesmerized by what they had seen, if they had not gone on to watch for what He would do next and be a part of it, then it would have been difficult for birth to be given to the New Testament church. The Lord wanted them to be involved with what He told them to do and then to wait and watch for His response, once again in His timeframe. This was but the beginning of the early church. They had to stand in faith and see what the Lord would do as they spread the gospel, wrote the Bible, stood in persecution, organized the church, and defined the boundaries of Christian doctrine. In later years, the early church fathers had to watch and see how the Lord would preserve His precious truth over the centuries against heretics, false prophets, and false teachers.

Watching Today

Nearly twenty centuries later, the Christian church still waits and watches to see what the Lord will do next. Sometimes, however, we have the idea that the main idea of watching is to find a hill someplace, stand there, and watch for the Lord's return, but this is a very narrow view of what the word *watch* signifies. Yes, the third watch may very well include the second return of Jesus Christ, and the midnight hour in which we now find ourselves may surely be the time, but the responsibility of the church is to continue to watch.

The Holy Spirit is very active today. Nations are being changed by the gospel message, by intercessory prayer teams, by mercy ministries, and by miraculous power encounters with the Holy Spirit. More Christians are being tortured and martyred than ever before but, at the same time, more people are coming to the Lord than ever before. Outreach ministries are uniting together to take the message to unreached people in the world. The gospel is being preached through radio, television, computers, books, tracts, and various other means. The church today has just entered a pivotal point in God's timetable and we must be watchful.

Amazing restoration of truth has transformed the church in the last few centuries. The restoration of truth—such as salvation by faith, water baptism, repentance, and methodical study of the Bible—acted as a foundation for the later restoration of things like healing, the laying on of hands, baptism of the Holy Spirit, and the gifts of the Holy Spirit. There has also been rediscovery of how the Bible says to set up church government with elders and deacons. The non-denominational movement has grown, as well as various denominations. The gifting of fivefold ministry of apostles, prophets, evangelists, pastors, and teachers (Ephesians 4:11-12) is once more recognized in many Christian circles as something for present-day ministry.

I have been at meetings with pastors from many denominational affiliations who were all raising their hands in praise to the Lord, while singing contemporary praise and worship songs penned by charismatic or Pentecostal songwriters. Many of these pastors were from conservative or fundamental Christian backgrounds. This was unheard of thirty years ago.

Some of the ministry events that have transpired in the United States in the last decade of the twentieth century are completely unparalleled in church history in regard to size. The Promise Keepers gathering in Washington D.C. was strengthened by more than one and a half million men praying for family and nation. The international gathering of clergy in Atlanta, Georgia, was close to 44,000 strong. Places like Toronto, Canada and Brownsville, Florida, received millions of travelers who wanted to see what the Holy Spirit was doing in those renewal centers.

Around the world, the Lord has been transforming various communities through citywide prayer meetings. Among Christians there is a growing sense of brotherhood and unity that crosses ethnic, cultural, and denominational lines. There are now mega-churches of tens or hundreds of thousands in many of the major cities of the world. New vision for training is also springing up, as local churches get more involved in mentoring and discipleship. Some have even begun training people for ministry within the four walls of the church rather than sending them off to four-year Bible colleges.

Watching the positive things that the Holy Spirit is doing in the church and the earth should be very exciting for Christians! Thus, learning to watch is important. Yet, there is only one thing that will make all of this pale in comparison, and that is the return of the Master to His servants.

Questions: For Study, Review and discussion

1. Do you consider yourself visually observant? How about spiritually observant? Are you able to patiently watch for what the Lord is doing?

2. Once Noah did all that the Lord requested of him, what was the only thing left for him to do? Have you stepped out on faith in such a way that all you could do was to watch what the Lord would do in response to your actions? Consider the illustration of the man who had faulty thinking about saving money and God's manner of provision. How can we avoid this type of thinking?

3. How did Abraham get ahead of God's timing? Have you ever gotten ahead of God's timing? The Lord is able to bypass our mistakes and make the best of our faults. Do you have any specific examples of this from your own life?

4. Discuss the difference between pondering and acting? What can we learn from the stories of Habakkuk and Joash?

5. The Lord's life, while on earth, was an amazing thing for the disciples to watch. What would have gone through your mind if you saw the things they did? What amazing things from God can we watch for today?

The Master of the Watching Servants

Victor Diaz watches for the Lord from Batopilas, a small community in Mexico that sits at the bottom of the Copper Canyon. The city of about 1200 Mexicans was once considered the second largest producer of silver in the world. Its remote location makes it a target area for cartels, which use Mexicans and the Tarahumara Indians from the surrounding mountains to work in secret fields harvesting drug crops. Victor is a simple, older man who makes his living doing various jobs for the villagers. About twenty years ago, while working on a bridge project, he received an injury which eventually led to his leg being amputated. Victor gave his life to Jesus years ago and, despite his hardships, has a positive faith in the Lord and His purposes. I met him while visiting with Fred and Nadia Warren, who were missionaries from our church sent to Batopilas. The Warrens are no longer missionaries in that city, but before they left they helped get a Bible study started that eventually became the only church in the city besides the Catholic one. Victor is now a part of that Christian church of believers and helps to be a light in a dark place by promoting Jesus and reaching out to destitute people with love and mercy.

The Wedding Ends

I am told that I used to be a head-banger when I was an infant. I loved to bang my head and sing myself to sleep. This might be inherent in my family as my son, Jonathan, and my brother's boys did the same thing. Weird!

Apparently, I liked to sit with my back to the glass picture tube on the front of my parent's black and white console television and bang my head against it. If I understand correctly, my parents ended up putting the T.V. (not me) inside the crib for nine months so that I would not hurt myself by breaking the glass. I could climb out of my crib but not into it, so the television and I were safe.

The other aspect of the banging was the singing. Actually, I liked to sing even without the banging. My favorite songs at age fourteen months were "Happy Birthday" and "Silent Night." I am sure I did not know many words to either one, just enough for people to recognize what I was singing. Since my birthday is the day after Christmas (I don't recommend it; it's a ripoff when it comes to presents), I attached great significance to these two songs and could be found joyfully humming or attempting the lyrics no matter where I was. From what I've heard, I guess people were pretty shocked at my cousin Mary's wedding when a fourteen-month-old toddler started singing "Happy Birthday" loud enough to disturb the ceremony.

Weddings hold great spiritual significance in Scripture. In the parable of the watching servants, we read that the master was away at a wedding (Luke 12:36). Weddings are usually joyful events, and I am sure that Jesus meant to convey this to the hearers of the parable. Let's read the parable again:

Let your waist be girded and your lamps burning; and you yourselves be like men who wait for *their master, when he will return from the wedding,* that when he comes and knocks they may open to him immediately. *Blessed are those servants* whom the master, when he comes, will find watching. Assuredly, I say to you that he will gird himself and have them sit down to eat, and will come and serve them. And if he should come in the second watch, or come in the third watch, and find them so, *blessed are those servants*
Luke 12:35-38, emphasis added

What wedding was this? Some might stop on this verse and wonder if this is none other than the great wedding of Christ with the church and marriage supper of the Lamb (Revelation 19), the final joy of the blessed as pictured in the parable of the ten virgins. But this is not that wedding. Since the parable of the watching servants itself is about the second coming of the Lord, and since the marriage of Jesus Christ to His church happens after His return, then this wedding must be a different one. Which one? Well, it would make sense that this is referring to Christ's session at the right hand of God between the times of His ascension from earth into heaven and when He will come again.

The key in regard to this wedding, however, is that it ends. The master eventually comes home to see what His servants are doing. Jesus will end His session at the right hand of God and return to the earth. Some people in the world don't realize this. Others who know about it don't believe it, but someday Jesus Christ is going to return, and all these atheists and agnostics will see that they were wrong. The people who served false gods will wish that they had not. Those who fought the gospel or persecuted the church will be ashamed. This is sad but true. The end is coming, and the Master will return. At that time, the saints will rejoice. There will be great jubilation! It will also be time for inspection. The Master will survey the house to see if the chores have been done.

Blessed Servants

In this passage, the servants who have performed the tasks, thus fulfilling the watch, are twice referred to as *blessed*. The word "blessed" comes from the Greek word *makarios* and means "supremely blessed, fortunate, well off" with the pure meaning being "the one on whom joy and grace outflows." Wow! I would like to be blessed in that sense. How about you? There is coming a day when the Lord Jesus will return and bestow great blessings upon His faithful servants.

What are some of those blessings? The Bible is rich with the subject of blessings. Throughout both Old and New Testaments we see the word *blessed* used numerous times in applications too time consuming for this brief study. But we can get a sense of the gravity of the impartation of His blessings in the Old Testament when we consider how He blessed His creation, the Sabbath day, the patriarchs and the children of Israel, and the life of King David. Many blessings are spoken of in Psalms and Proverbs.

The New Testament also contains examples of blessings which help to increase our understanding of our future blessing. In the Sermon on the Mount, Jesus pronounced the blessings for those who portrayed various godly characteristics. The rewards include comfort, mercy, fulfillment, being called sons of God, inheriting the earth, entrance into heaven, and seeing God (Matthew 5:3-10). This is pretty amazing stuff, but the New Testament doesn't stop there. The faithful servants of the Lord shall also be made rulers over all of the Lord's goods (Matthew 24:46-47) and have access to the tree of life in the city of God (Revelation 22:14).

It is interesting to note that the Master Jesus blessed His followers just as He was actually ascending into heaven and this produced in them worship, great joy, and the praising and blessing of God (Luke 24:51-53). When He returns, He is looking to reward His faithful, watching servants with great blessings.

Parables of Warning

The Bible does not teach that all those called *servants* will be in good standing with the Master when He returns. This should be a sober warning for Christians and produce the fear of the Lord, thus purifying motives. After the parable of the watching servants in Luke, Jesus goes on to explain that the Master may come and find His servants not doing what they are supposed to be doing. These will receive punishment.

Luke 12:42-46 contrasts servants (leaders) who are faithful and those who are not. Verses 45-46 refer to the unfaithful servant:

> If that servant says in his heart, "My Master is delaying his coming," and begins to beat the male and female servants, and to eat and drink and be drunk, the master of that servant will come on a day when he is not looking for him, and at an hour when he is not aware, and will cut him in two and appoint him his portion with the unbelievers.

I'll let the reader draw his own conclusions about the state of salvation of this individual. All I know is that I would not want to be in his shoes. This should act as an exhortation to those who are considered Christian leaders today to be expectant of the Master's coming, to be kind to those who serve alongside or underneath, and to have integrity of character.

Furthermore, Luke 12:47-48 goes on to explain that the servants will be held accountable for what they know and do not do and will receive beatings for their lack of faithfulness:

> And that servant who knew his master's will, and did not prepare himself or do according to his will, shall be beaten with many stripes. But he who did not know, yet committed things deserving of stripes, shall be beaten with few. For everyone to whom much is given, from him much will be required; and to whom much has been committed, of him they will ask the more.

There are two different levels of punishment given to these servants. The one who knows his master's will and does not do it receives more punishment than the one who is unaware of his master's will. This is certainly fair, yet it is probably hard for Christians to imagine their loving Savior Jesus Christ beating anyone. We don't know what these beatings symbolize—if they are actual physical beatings, or if they represent the natural things that beat upon a Christian's life when he or she knows better but does not walk in the principles of God. This concept might find a parallel in 1 Corinthians 3:12-15 in which some build their lives with wood, hay, and straw and suffer loss but are saved "through fire."

Perhaps there is another explanation. Isaiah 53 refers to the suffering of Jesus on our behalf. He suffered on the cross for each one of our sins. In verse 5 it says that "by His stripes we are healed." Jesus received many beatings for us. Peter expounds on this, writing, "Who Himself bore our sins on the tree, that we, having died to sins, might live for righteousness—by whose stripes you were healed" (1 Peter 2:24). Could it be that Jesus has already taken the stripes or beatings for each of these unfaithful servants? Perhaps the punishment will be an understanding of how much Jesus had to suffer for each of them because of their lack in following the will of the Lord.

In reality we might all be deserving of a certain amount of stripes if our faithfulness were measured against that of the perfect One—Jesus. Perhaps when He comes, each of us will be given a glimpse of what He suffered on our behalf. He is the only One who knows the difference between our faithfulness and that which we have lacked, causing us to be so very grateful and full of love for the blessed eternity He offers us.

Of course, this is all conjecture, and none of us may really know the significance of these verses regarding the punishment of unfaithful servants until the Lord comes. But this passage should remind Christians that God is holy and just, and that we are instructed throughout Scripture to serve Him with a measure of reverential fear.

The Master Serves the Servants

The Lord is worthy of all praise and reverence. There is no one else like Him. What master actually takes the time to serve his own servants? And yet, that is what the Master Jesus did when He washed the disciples' feet and that is what He will do when He comes again. He will take time to serve His servants.

In the parable of the watching servants, after the master pronounces blessing upon the faithful, he comes to them and serves them. We have such an incredible Master, that when He returns, we will sit and dine at the table as He serves us. The Master will gird His robe and then bid the servants to sit down and eat.

On one hand, it is amazing to think that Jesus will come and serve us. But, on the other hand, it should not be so amazing. It is in such a manner that He came and served His followers the first time. As a matter of fact, He serves us constantly! The following verses portray a similar setting and show a connection with the parable of the watching servants:

> The kings of Gentiles exercise lordship over them, and those who exercise authority over them are called benefactors. But not so among you; on the contrary, he who is greatest among you, let him be as the younger, and he who governs as he who serves. *For who is greater, he who sits at the table, or he who serves? Is it not he who sits at the table? Yet I am among you as one who serves.* But you are those who have continued with Me in My trials. And I bestow upon you a kingdom, just as My Father bestowed one upon Me, *that you may eat and drink at My table in My kingdom*, and sit on thrones judging the twelve tribes of Israel
> LUKE 22:25-30, EMPHASIS ADDED

There are a couple of similarities in this passage and the parable quoted before. One, as mentioned, is in the area of the Lord serving His people. Once again, this is an example for us in the modern-day church. Leaders should be servants and lead by example. Another thing that the two parables share in common is the idea of eating at the table of the Lord.

It would make sense that both the passages from Luke 12:35-38 (the parable of the watching servants) and the one above from Luke 22:25-30 are illustrating the marriage supper of the Lamb expounded upon in Revelation 19. This is the time when Christians will enter into the joy of the Lord, the moment that we anticipate and for which we hope. The Master's servants will be properly rewarded for their faithfulness in performing the tasks and watching for His return.

Summary

We have learned about the parable of the watching servants. We know that the master represents Jesus and the servants, Christians. Jesus will return from His session at the right hand of God, which is illustrated by His attendance at the wedding. The heart of a servant is one of humility, with a desire to please the Master Jesus. The servants are asked to do several tasks. They are to 1) have their waists girded, 2) have their lamps burning, 3) be waiting, and 4) open immediately to the master's knock. The combination of these tasks performed actually helps define for us what it means for these servants to watch. Each of these tasks has symbolism that relates to our daily lives as Christians. We are to become disciples (disciplined) and mature while, at the same time, learn to serve. We should share the light of Christ and wait patiently for the Master's return.

There is a great need to learn to watch. Sometimes we can merely ponder as we watch what the Lord is doing. We are being schooled. At other times, we must become involved with His projects and then watch what He will do. When the Master finally comes, He will invite us to be seated at His table and He will serve us. This represents the final joy of the blessed and the marriage supper of the Lamb. Now let's consider the church of the third watch.

QUESTIONS: FOR STUDY, REVIEW AND DISCUSSION

1. In the parable of the watching servants, Jesus is represented by the master who returns from a wedding. What does this wedding probably represent?

2. Define the word "blessed." Who will receive the blessing from the Master? What are some of the blessings that the Lord gives now and some of those promised to His servants when He comes?

3. Discuss the parables dealing with warning. What happened to the unfaithful servants or those who took advantage of the other servants? How do these apply to our lives as Christians? What are some of the various things that the "stripes" might signify?

4. Consider how the master will serve the servants at the table. What do you get out of this? What does the meal represent? How does the Lord already serve His servants?

5. Read the parable of the watching servants again. Prayerfully consider if the Lord is speaking to you about any area of service in which He is calling you to excel?

PART THREE

THE CHURCH OF THE THIRD WATCH

THE CHURCH IN TRANSITION

Ralph and Judi Wright watch for the Lord from Tornillo, Texas where they operate a home for special needs children. New Life Home is located on the border of Mexico and Texas, allowing the couple to minister on both sides of the border. Ralph and Judi, formerly from northern Idaho, felt called to go to Texas several years ago, along with their twelve adopted special needs children and some natural ones, to take charge of a ministry for children. Their ministry of mercy not only extends to special needs children from various countries and ethnic backgrounds, but they have developed outreaches to parents of special needs children, orphanages in Mexico, hungry people in the El Paso area, and missionaries in transit. Along with this, they are involved in a local Hispanic church pastored by Victor Franco, called Temple Shalom that is very outgoing and ministry–related. The uniqueness of the Wright's ministry has opened doors with the social services throughout El Paso and given them a voice into the lives of many hurting people needing to hear about Jesus the Great Healer. It always amazes me that Ralph and Judi can stay calm, peaceful, and reliant upon the Lord for His strength and guidance in the midst of daily caring for the children, and being involved in many types of ministry activity.

The Charge to the Church

The church must receive the lamp of truth from the past, shine it into the present darkness so that people can watch, and relay it on into the hands of the future generation.

I once envisioned a line of men representing the generations of the church. These men reminded me of a painting by Michelangelo. Each man reached backward with one arm extended to the hand of the man behind him and reached forward with the other arm to the hand of the man in front of him. The head of each individual was transitional and changing from looking back to the man in the past, to looking sideways and focused on the present, to looking forward to the man in the future. Almost like runners handing off a baton, each generation was passing off the charge of the church to the future generation by the touch of hands. Each saw what was behind, before, and beyond. The face of each individual was also transitional and changing from a boy looking backwards to an adult male looking sideways to an aged man looking ahead to the boy in front of him.

The church is always in transition. Change is inevitable. Our generation—our watch—must carry the light forward and shine it about into the darkness to help people see the Way and then pass it on into the capable hands of the upcoming generation. We can do no more. Heaven help us to do no less!

No one but God has a grasp on the entirety of the church in the earth. Who even comes close to knowing how many saints pass on into glory everyday hoping that they have impacted the next generation of Christians in a positive, fruitful way? How many new converts are daily beginning their journey into discipleship? How many backslide or repent? Where is growth the most fruitful and lasting? Where are laborers needed the most? Which harvest field is the ripest? How many saints are faithfully working where they should? How many are like Jonah, running from the call? Statistics are great, but they only go so far. Only God really knows the hearts and answers.

Some Christians impact many, others only a few, but God sees the importance of each servant where He places them or—as the Bible illustrates—He sees the necessity of each part of His entire body, whether they be fingers, hands, joints, toes, feet, eyes, hearts, and so on (see 1 Corinthians 12). All are connected and important to the support and health of the body, but Christ is the head (Colossians 1:18). He knows where every member is and what needs to occur in the church of the third watch.

We are the servants at the very beginning of the third watch. Our generation might well be the ones who witness the second coming of the Lord, or it might be our children's generation. We really don't know. We might hope for it and believe it, yet, our charge is to loyally carry our lamp and serve the next generation by handing it off faithfully. We can do great evangelism exploits, create seeker-sensitive worship services, have the slickest church programs, speak statements about moral integrity, try to change laws in our country, as well as a host of other "good" things, but if we fail to relay the lamp of truth to the next generation, or if we drop it in the handoff, we have failed.

It is obvious that there are many challenges facing the church of the third watch. This chapter can mention just a few, and those only briefly, compared to what could be written because of the enormity of the task. However, through the discharge of the following eight topics, the lamp of truth will be passed on.

1: The Loving Church

Keeping our "first love" fresh and alive for the Lord is something we should always be concerned about. The church of Ephesus was commended for many things but then warned that they had left their first love. If they did not repent, the Lord would come and remove their lamp stand (Revelation 2:4-5).

Relaying to the future church a passion for God is perhaps first and foremost of all the things that we need to dispatch. The greatest commandment is to love God with all of our heart, soul, strength, and mind (Luke 10:27). Along with this commandment is that we are to love our neighbor as ourselves. Much of this love can be extended to the community from the church via compassionate ministries. Ways to reach out with love are too numerous to mention, but the truth of these must be passed on to the hands of the next generation.

2: The Gospel Bearing Church

It cannot be stated too emphatically that the lamp of truth to be passed on must include the gospel message. Second Corinthians 4:4 calls it "the light of the gospel of the glory of Christ." Paul and the other apostles fought against heresy when gnosticism tried to creep into the early church. People from various heretic groups taught about "another Jesus," a "different spirit," and a "different gospel" (2 Corinthians 11:4). John tells us that there were those who denied that Jesus Christ came in the flesh (John 4:3) and some who do not "abide in the doctrine of Christ" (2 John 9), while Paul wrote to the Galatians about their false gospel of works. He outlined the basic gospel message for us in 1 Corinthians 15:1-8. It is the Good News of Jesus Christ coming to die for our sins on the cross, being buried, and then resurrected on the third day, the message of John 3:16 that has changed lives for over 2,000 years.

There are those today who deny the deity of Jesus Christ, the fact that He ever came in the flesh, or that He arose from the dead in a physical body. Some say He was a good teacher but not God incarnate. Others challenge the substitutionary atonement of Christ on the cross for sinners. They cannot comprehend how His shed blood cleanses from "all sin" (1 John 1:7) and so, not understanding it, they deny it. We know that to many the "message of the cross is foolishness" (1 Corinthians 1:18), but for those who believe "it is the power of God to salvation" (Romans 1:16).

As servants of the third watch, we must serve the next generation by training them in the gospel. Too often do teachers forget to include the gospel in their messages, seeking instead to speak "feel good" words that entice the ears but miss the weightier matters of how Jesus suffered and why we can be free from sin. Cultures may change, and even the method of transmission, but the truth of the gospel must be relayed.

3: The Praying Church

In the garden of Gethsemane, Jesus told Peter, James, and John to *watch* and to *pray*. The word *watch* here simply means to stay awake and be vigilant. Three times Jesus went off by Himself to pray and returned only to find them sleeping (see Matthew 26:36-46). The first time He returned He said to Peter, "What! Could you not watch with Me one hour? Watch and pray, lest you enter into temptation. The spirit indeed is willing, but the flesh is weak" (verses 40-41). Perhaps Jesus was warning Peter here because he had made such a bold profession of faith about never denying Jesus, just prior to the garden incident (verse 34).

Of course, Peter did end up denying Jesus three times that night but later repented and became a great apostle of the New Testament church. It was probably the Gethsemane experience in Peter's life that caused him to eventually exhort other followers, writing that "The end of all things is at hand; therefore be serious and *watchful in your prayers*" (1 Peter 4:7, emphasis added). Paul, when writing to the Ephesians, said as much: "*praying always with all prayer* and supplication in the Spirit, *being watchful* to this end with all perseverance and supplication for all the saints" (Ephesians 6:18, emphasis added).

The church of the third watch needs to serve the next generation by teaching them to be watchful in their prayers. The word *pray* or *prayer* is used 127 times in the New Testament, giving information on how to pray, what to pray, when to pray, and even on praying in tongues when we don't know what to pray or in times of dryness. Our prayers should be watchful, not always looking inward with a "bless-me" list, but looking towards God, asking Him for guidance in what He wants us to pray. We are to be alert and vigilant in our prayer efforts, knowing that our time is limited and Christ's return is certain.

The church needs to encourage both individual and corporate times of prayer. Already pastors are praying together, Christians are praying for lost peoples and societies, and cities and countries are being changed through the dynamics of prayer. The next generation cannot just be *taught* about prayer. They need to learn to commune with the Spirit in prayer; they must learn to carry the lamp of truth and to pray. As the expression goes, "Some things are better caught than taught" and prayer needs to be caught. Teaching on prayer is necessary so that people don't get off base, but it must be experienced and embraced as well. Otherwise, the handoff from one generation to the next will be incomplete.

4: The Worshiping Church

The Father is seeking people who will worship Him in spirit and truth (see John 4:23). People worship the Lord by numerous means, but whether in song, prayer, meditation, hearing the Word preached, congregational reading of the Word, or communion, it should be done in spirit and truth.

What will we pass on to the next generation? Hopefully, it will be a desire of the heart to worship the Lord in spirit and truth. Today, we see much contemporary Christian praise and worship music whose words are often very complicated. While it is awesome to see a spiritual type of David's Tabernacle (Acts 15:16-17) being restored to the church with respect to praise and worship, there must be a balance that accompanies the movement. Otherwise, we may create worship teams that are technically talented but miss the heart of the Spirit in worship. We create praise songs that are so complex, people can't memorize them quickly enough to forget about the words and focus on the Lord while singing. Also, the songs need to have scriptural accuracy. We don't want people singing faulty theology or even subjective lyrics that focus on "me" rather than on God. Some songs today seem to glorify self over Jesus Christ.

Congregations have various styles of worship, thus attracting and reaching various groups of people. The next generation will also expand and develop new styles of music. This is to be expected. Liturgies, hymns, and choruses are not for everyone, but what must be passed on is a heart for true worship and not just a heart for singing or technical skill.

5: The Visionary Church

The writer of Proverbs tells us that "where there is no vision, the people perish" (29:18 KJV). Congregations that lack inspired purpose or vision stumble around trying to figure out what to do. The word "vision" in this Scripture refers to either divine revelation or the faithful preaching of the Word. If these things are lacking, surely doom is in the forecast. There needs to be both the prophetic ministry and the preaching of the solid Word. The prophetic word brings edification, exhortation, comfort (1 Corinthians 14:3), as well as other directive words by seasoned prophets that the church needs. It must always be in line with the Bible, however, not the other way around, or it is rejected.

I would also remind the reader that when I received the vision of the third watch there were several areas I felt impressed about concerning the church. We need to: 1) fervently maintain and upgrade our watch for the return of the Lord, 2) guard the borders of Christianity against heresy, and 3) extend God's kingdom throughout the world. These three areas need to be preached as they help give definition to the vision to be cast before congregations. It is the responsibility of this generation to watch for the Lord, guard the borders of Christianity, and extend the kingdom of God. When Christians live with the foundational hope of Christ's return, build their lives on the solid doctrine of God's Word, and reach out to others in a lost and dying world, this is truly visionary.

6: The Character-Driven Church

God is more interested in righteous character than talent. We have already discussed this in Chapter Five, but it is worth mentioning again. Churches need to emphasize righteous character over any gifts, talents, wealth, or intelligence. Leaders should have the character of elders and deacons (1 Timothy 3:1-13; Titus 1:5-9).

People or churches that are considered gossip centers should be challenged and changed. Offenses need to be worked out in a fair and biblical manner, and moral integrity, pure motives, and genuine honesty should be the norm. Children that grow up seeing hypocrisy may reject their parent's religion and the lamp will fall to the ground. We must give the next generation an ethical compass concerning things like cloning, euthanasia, abortion, homosexuality, occult activities, and false doctrines. The issues they face may be far more threatening to the church at large than the things we have faced. Righteous character needs to be taught, caught, sought, and bought. It is indispensable.

7: The Discerning Church

Not every one who calls himself a Christian is one. Not every one who says Jesus is his Lord lives up to that profession. Through the years, I have been curious how some people can give their name for membership in a church without having accepted Jesus as Savior and Lord. Have you ever met anybody like this? These people have missed the basic point of Christianity. Unless one is redeemed through a personal relationship with Jesus Christ, there is no true belonging to Him or His church. Simply going to a church building may make one *appear* religious, but it doesn't necessarily make him a part of the true global Christian church. John 17:3 tells us, "This is eternal life, that they may know You, the only true God, and Jesus Christ whom You have sent."

According to Hebrews 5:14, a major part of gaining discernment comes by feeding on the Word of God. We must help generate an intense hunger for the Word in the next generation. We need people of the Word who "have their senses exercised to discern both the good and evil." There are deceivers outside the church—and sometimes within— and the next generation needs capable discerning leaders. The Bible warns us about false prophets and teachers within the borders of Christianity who exploit Christians with deceptive words but actually deny the Lord (2 Peter 2:1-3), as well as others who creep into the midst of the saints having impure, lewd motives (Jude 4). Jesus even warned that there would be many over the ages of time that would use His Word as a tool for prophecy, deliverance, and attention-getting wonders, but who would *not* truly know Him in their own hearts (Matthew 7:22-23).

We also know that the Lord warned us about false christs (Matthew 24:24) and deceiving spirits and doctrines of demons (1 Timothy 4:1) in these last days. Furthermore, as one who has extensively studied and written on the subject of cults and world religions, I am amazed at just how many people are following fables (2 Timothy 4:4), dead works, and doing religious works without any real relationship with God.

On my first trip to the Philippines, I encountered two Mormon missionaries from the States who were enticed by an evangelistic drama that our mission team was putting on in the park. I have a heart for Mormons. I don't slam the door in their face or pull the blinds and hide in fear. They need to be reached with the true gospel and the true Jesus. So, I went over to them, introduced myself, and spent some time witnessing to these two young men. The Lord opened their ears to me as I showed them the fallacy of the Book of Mormon and their doctrines. I shared my testimony and the truth about what the Bible says about Jesus, as compared to their false concept of Him.

One of my co-workers asked if they understood what I was saying. They responded, "Yes." Then he asked them, "Do you believe it?" We were both a little shocked when they said, "It sounded accurate and true." So Don pressed them a little more and said, "Well, if you believe it, what is to stop you right now from accepting the Jesus of the Bible as your Lord and Savior and denouncing the things about Mormonism that you know are not true?" One of the Mormon missionaries gave a response that we will not soon forget. He told us that if he did this, his family, friends, and girlfriend would disown him. He would not get the summer job promised to him upon his return, and he would not receive a college scholarship for the following fall's semester. Talk about pressure! The missionaries left, and we prayed for them. Perhaps someday God will use the seeds planted to bring them into His truth of Christianity, making them a part of the true global church.

It probably won't surprise anyone that I take issue with the view of some American Christians who think that the American church shouldn't be sending missionaries to the foreign fields because we have enough of our own problems or because we haven't yet reached our own Jerusalem and Samaria first. While there is a measure of truth to this, it can also be an excuse for not getting involved. The fact is, our American culture is exporting homegrown cults into the world harvest fields. Hopefully, Christians can do more than the cults in sending out the truth of the Bible to the other cultures and people groups of the world!

8: The Disciple-Making Church

The passing of the lamp of truth to the next generation basically means making them disciples to carry on the work and hand down the lamp to their children and grandchildren. I think it is interesting that Jesus said in what we call the great commission to "make disciples" (Matthew 28:19). The emphasis wasn't on evangelism. That is taken for granted. But the necessity is in making disciples. This we must do if we are to fulfill His command. We must be disciples, and we must make disciples.

How about you? Are you a disciple of Jesus Christ? Have you chosen to follow Jesus Christ? Have you turned from your ways to His ways? Have you accepted Him as your Savior and your Lord? If your answer to these questions is "yes," then you are a part of the true global church. You are a *called-out one*, and He has a plan and purpose for your life. A part of that plan is for you to grow in understanding of the times that are at hand, and in preparation for service because you are a servant of the third watch.

Putting All the Pieces Together

My mom was an expert at jigsaw puzzles. I don't know how she ever had the patience for it, but she would empty out 5,000 pieces of a puzzle on a card table and spend many hours sorting out the pieces by color, shape, and pattern. Then she would put together all the straight pieces until she had completed the borders. From this point, she still had much to accomplish, but she would carefully fit pieces together by design and color, making trees or rivers or whatever picturesque scenes the puzzle portrayed. When I asked her why she did it, her reply was simply, "I like to do it. It brings me pleasure."

Somehow the Lord will put all the pieces together in the right places to build His church. He is the Master Puzzle Solver. He knows how to take opposing ends and funny-looking pieces and put them all together into a picture of beauty. No harm intended but, in my analogy, Christians are the funny-looking pieces. The opposing ends represent the many differing views within Christianity that all seem to find their source in Scripture.

The pieces of the puzzle certainly have limited perspective compared to the puzzle builder. The Lord is putting all the pieces together today in perfect harmony. The individual pieces might not see it nor comprehend it, but God has His plan. He is building His church, and nothing will prevail against it. The day will come when the Master Puzzle Builder will complete the perfect puzzle.

Questions: For Study, Review and discussion

1. Consider the illustration of the generations as a line of men reaching backward with one hand and forward with the other to the generations. With this in mind, what do you think the main charge is to the present-day church?

2. Discuss what the past church generation passed on and what the current generation needs to pass on to the next. What are things that we need to change in the current generation?

3. I listed eight charges in the chapter. The first three are: (1) the loving church, (2) the gospel-bearing church, and (3) the praying church. Is one of these more important than the other two or than all the rest? Consider the church charges in regard to past, present, and future. Were these passed on from past church generations? How is the present-day church doing with these? How can we effectively hand them off to the next generation?

4. The next three charges listed are: (4) the worshiping church, (5) the visionary church, and (6) the character-driven church. What are some major issues in worship that the present-day church is dealing with? How about vision and character? What do we need to pass on?

5. Consider the topics of (7) discernment and (8) disciple making. How should we approach training the next generation in order to equip them to discern and hold on to the lamp of Christian truth?

CHAPTER TEN

LOOK WHO'S WATCHING THE CHURCH

Dennis and Kathy Balcombe watch for the Lord from Hong Kong, China. They pastor Revival Christian Church in Hong Kong and have helped develop Revival Chinese Ministries International, which has branches in various countries with outreach ministries to the Chinese. Hundreds of short-term and long-term missionaries venture to Hong Kong every year to smuggle Bibles and teaching aids across the main border through a ministry called Donkeys for Jesus. These books are then distributed throughout China to the millions of waiting Christians who have no Bibles of their own. According to Dennis, there is a large problem with numerous cults spreading various false doctrines, but the growth in Christian converts is such that the lack of Bibles is very unfortunate. Today, it is estimated that over a hundred million Chinese are Christians. Because of the limitations by the government on Christian gatherings, they are forced to meet in parks, homes, or caves rather than church buildings. The persecution is great in China, but so are the miraculous signs and wonders of those following the Lord. The Holy Spirit is doing marvelous wonders. Dennis and Kathy have seen great numbers of Chinese come to the Lord through their ministry. They are sold out for the Lord in China and hope for a greater harvest before the day of His return.

A Light Set Upon a Hill

One summer when I was a teenager and on staff at a Boy Scout camp in northern California, I was walking along the trail around a lake in the dark, remembering my way back to the council fire. I knew the trail by heart after many weeks of using it. Suddenly a bright strobe light flashed in my face, momentarily shocking and disorienting me. I actually fell down by the blast of that light on my eyes. Then I heard laughing and cracking in the woods as a friend of mine ran back to the fire, knowing he had gotten me really good. After I regained my sight and composure, I edged my way along the trail, on guard against other assaults, until I saw the firelight growing with the steps of my approach. That light was a pleasure to my senses as my eyes grew accustomed to it, and I could gradually discern the world around me. The one light hurt my eyes while the other one helped me to better see the things around me.

It is not always easy as Christians to know how we should share the light of Christ with others. I think most of us would prefer not to use the shocking strobe light that knocks others off their feet, disorientating them. There may be times when the Lord would use this method to get someone's attention, as in the case of Saul on the road to Damascus. However, when most Christians reflect on their own conversion journey, they remember a gradual change in their view of God, the world, and self. Their spiritual blindness was healed as the eyes of their hearts began to steadily adjust to the truth of Jesus.

Of course, not everyone wants the light turned on because they are evil and the light exposes their evil deeds. Jesus said, "Men loved darkness rather than light, because their deeds were evil" (John 3:19). He went on in that passage to contrast evil and truth. Those who do truth come to the light that their deeds may be clearly seen.

People are attracted to light in the lives of Christians and in the life of the church. This book so far has been concerned with the need for Christians to be watchful servants, but we must also realize that others—who need what we have—are watching the church. Does our Christian light help them to see the truth, or does it hurt their eyes?

The lonely, the hurting, the broken, the needy, the outcast, and the discouraged look about in a dark world and see a light shining upon a hill. Everything before has been darkness but now they gradually adjust their eyes and can discern a path up the hill to the light and they come. Remember what Jesus said to His followers:

> You are the light of the world. A city that is set on a hill cannot be hidden. Nor do they light a lamp and put it under a basket, but on a lampstand, and it gives light to all who are in the house. Let your light so shine before men, that they may see your good works and glorify your Father in heaven
> MATTHEW 5:14-16

Those in distress, who humble themselves and look upward to the God of heaven, become aware of a light upon a hill. The church, even with all of its problems past and present, can be a safe haven for world-worn travelers.

I am glad to be a Christian and a follower of Jesus Christ. I can testify of numerous men and women, both young and old, who passionately love God, who care about others, and who want to see people come into the kingdom of God and be healed. These people live by a code of Christian principles. No, they are not perfect, nor do they claim to be. They simply know that they need a Savior and so does everyone else. They know the Savior and His name is Jesus. They know His Word and it is the Bible. They try to shine their light the best way possible in the situations they encounter. Of course, some must learn not to hide their lamps under a basket. Others need to back off a bit from the strobe-light approach. That is all a part of becoming a disciple and learning to be a wise servant.

When Christians truly get a revelation of being a servant of Jesus Christ, they suddenly realize that the circumstances they are in can become God-appointed moments for the building of righteous character and the sharing of the light which they have found in Christ. Perhaps they will share His peace with others in the midst of great trials, or His love at a time of tremendous hurt, or His grace at moments of weakness. God's servants can be found in many nations involved in numerous tasks and experiences. Some might be found washing dishes in a restaurant, who see the needs of those around them and lovingly influence as many as they can for Christ. Maybe they are housewives raising a righteous seed, or entrepreneurs trying to finance kingdom efforts. They might be preaching from a pulpit, leading a small group, shining shoes in an airport, working in a lumber mill, going to college, or tending to the needs of dying loved ones. The Master has His servants in many parts of the house shining their lamps for others to see.

We serve an awesome Master, a great King, and a loving Savior. No one cares more for people than God. No one is more merciful. No one is fairer. His ways are righteous and beyond reproach. As my former pastor once said, "If people really knew God, they would love God."

However, in the history of Christianity, there is a list of myriad hurts and grievances leveled against Christians and congregations. Unfortunately, people throughout the ages have been hurt by various Christians or congregations so they have rejected God's people and, oftentimes, God Himself. Sometimes those who call themselves followers of Christ have done terrible things to others, and even said it was in the name of the Lord. Of course, it is not God doing these negative things, but their actions cause their victims to flee without giving the Lord Jesus a real chance. Then there are those who reject any kind of true discipleship in their lives. If any pastor or leader attempts to bring even loving correction and counsel, they flee, crying "legalism" or "control."

Even with the many problems within and without, however, the church is called to be a servant to God for the benefit of people—those who want the light of His truth. Societies are watching the church, communities are watching the church, and your neighbors are watching the church. Let's be sensitive to them and help them see the truth around them in a loving and merciful way.

Angels Watching Over Us

Most Christians recognize that there are angels watching over them. As a matter of fact, a lot of people who are not even Christians believe in this concept. But for Christians, the thought that a holy angel is watching over him or her is usually perceived as a positive and normal part of our spiritual experience.

God uses His angels to carry out His purposes on the earth. They may come to bring judgment as in the book of Revelation where angels are pouring out vials of the wrath of God on unredeemed people (Revelation 16). They are also involved with bringing revelation, help, warning, and other messages from God to His people. An example of angelic revelation is in the story of the angel giving Daniel prophetic vision (10:11). The apostle Peter was freed from jail through the miraculous help of an angel (Acts 12:7). We also see angels warning Lot and his family in Sodom (Genesis 19:12).

The Bible informs us that God uses angels to minister to those "who will inherit salvation" (Hebrews 1:14). To minister is to serve. He uses angels to serve those who are inheriting salvation. The following passage shows some aspects of that service:

> For He shall give His angels charge over you, to keep you in all your ways. In their hands they shall bear you up, lest you dash your foot against a stone
>
> PSALM 91:11-12

This charge to the angels is for direction and protection. They are to direct Christians into the ways of the Lord, and they are to give protection against harm and temptation. As a matter of fact, the devil used a perverted form of this passage to tempt Jesus to jump from the temple pinnacle (Matthew 4:6). But Jesus responded to the devil by saying, "You shall not tempt the Lord your God" (verse 7). Angels do not control Christians nor do they alter the free will of those who give into temptation and sin, but they will definitely warn and direct us into the right way for our lives and, by extension, into the purposes of God. Angels, acting as God's heavenly servants, are in the know concerning His plans and His timing.

It is also interesting that an angelic intermediary has a role in delivering the prayers of the saints before the throne of God in heaven just prior to the judgments sounded by the seven trumpets. In Revelation 8:3-4 an angel is offering incense along with the "prayers of the saints" on the altar before God. To God, our prayers are like a sweet smelling aroma (Psalm 141:2; Revelation 5:8). Furthermore, we see an angel bringing a message from God to Zachariah during the hour of incense and prayer, saying that Zachariah's prayer had been heard and that his wife, Elizabeth, would bear a son in old age and they would name him John.

The point of this is that angels are interested in, and at times involved in, a believer's prayer life. How they might work in conjunction with the influence of the Holy Spirit in a Christian's prayer life would make an interesting study, but my purpose here is to simply illustrate that angels are involved with Christians. They are not only watching *over* us, they are watching us. I am sure they are rooting us on to pray, to have faith, to trust in God, to do what is right, to share the gospel, and to be lights in a dark world.

It is comforting to know that angels are watching the church and spurring it on towards God's final glorious destiny for it, but it must also be remembered that God is interested in the cleansing and purity of His people and the church. If necessary, He will send correction, chastisement, or even judgment. Examples of this are seen in Revelation, chapters 2 and 3, in which the Lord sent messages to the angels over seven churches. Some people think the word "angel" in these passages were not heavenly beings but human messengers of God, perhaps the pastors of those churches. This may be true, but the real point is that God saw some things wrong with the church, and He was going to deal with it.

God will send loving correction and strict discipline to His children if that is what is needed. He may even do so with non-believers. In the process, He might use angels that are watching. Considering angels as watchers gives us another insight into some of the activity of the angelic holy ones. Look at how God dealt with King Nebuchadnezzar of Babylon. The king was unaware that angels were watching him and everything he did. He boasted and proclaimed the advancements of his kingdom by his own power, not giving any credit to God.

These watchers, who had been given authority by God, made a decree sentencing the king to a period of insanity in which he would become like a beast of the field. He was driven from men to the wilds of nature where he ate grass like a steer. When his faculties finally returned, he was humbled and, looking up to heaven, he gave honor and glory to God (Daniel 4). While we must remember that King Nebuchadnezzar was not a servant of God when this happened to him, it must also be conceded that God will deal with sin wherever He finds it.

As stated above, the king was totally unaware of the watchers. Christians today are also not always aware of the fact that we are being watched, but when we do remember it, we should know that it is not only for our protection and safety, but for our own good. The reality of it is that we probably behave better as a result of knowing that we are watched in our private, non-peopled moments.

The holy angels of God are not to be feared or worshiped by God's people (Revelation 22:9). Also, we are not to pray to them (Colossians 2:18). As mentioned earlier, they are serving those of us who are "inheriting salvation" (Hebrews 1:13), and they rejoice over even one sinner who repents (Luke 15:10). We admire their steadfastness with God and are grateful for their faithfulness to serve us. Who knows how many times our lives have been invisibly touched and encouraged by angelic fellow-servants of God! They watch as directed by God, and they watch over us.

The Great Watchman

The Lord is watching over His church. Jesus told us that in His Father's house there are many mansions. He went to prepare a place for us, and one day He will come again and receive us (John 14:3). In Scripture Jesus is symbolized as a type of the groom and the church as His bride. In Revelation 19, we see the "marriage supper of the lamb" at which the bride "has made herself ready" and is dressed "in fine linen, clean and bright" representing the righteous acts of the saints.

In conjunction with this, God is sanctifying and cleansing the church (His bride) through the Holy Spirit "that He might present her to Himself a glorious church, not having spot or wrinkle or any such thing, but that she be holy and without blemish" (Ephesians 5:27). The passage surrounding this verse also emphasizes God's great love for the bride whom He nourishes and cherishes.

God will not tarry forever. He will one day return for His bride. For now, however, He is patiently waiting for men to repent and to come to the knowledge of salvation. He is equipping His church through the Holy Spirit to reach all the nations of the world with the glorious light of the gospel.

The Watchman's Clock

It cannot be denied that we live in amazing days. God's clock is ticking down to the time of His Son's return. The church looks much different after the 2,000 years since its inception. The last century beheld the development of a great global awareness of the church. Mass communication via radio, television, satellites, computer, and publishing has greatly increased the potential for fulfilling the goal of the great commission. Two world wars and the creation of nuclear warheads brought visions of Armageddon. The end of the twentieth century saw an increase in terrorism throughout the world and in the United States. Now that we have entered the new millennium, the threat has even increased!

Terrorists attacked the United States on September 11, 2001, when suicide hijackers stole four airline passenger jets. Three of these, they successfully used as flying bombs, crashing two of them into the twin towers of the World Trade Center in New York City and another one into the Pentagon in Washington D.C. Passenger-heroes overcame the hijackers on the fourth plane, and it was forced to crash outside of Pittsburgh, Pennsylvania. Thousands were killed as we faced the second greatest attack within the borders of our country since Pearl Harbor. Suddenly, in that one day, the world changed. All of us in America were mourning and praying, and many nations showed their support by doing the same. At the same time, people in hostile nations were dancing in the streets celebrating our hurt.

It is at a time like this that some will sound alarmist trumpets, project defeat for the church, or portray escapist attitudes in desiring a quick rapture. But such thinking should be weighed against the need for positive, victorious, overcoming, watchman faith. It is not time to run and hide in fear. It is time to stand up and serve. Yes, we must man our posts and be watchful for the Lord, but we must also serve the church and raise up the next generation. God still wants to bring many more people into His church. We must train them to have discernment of the times, and we must impart the many charges listed in the last chapter.

We are the servants of the third watch, and we have entered the midnight hour. There is no mistake about it, this is the time predicted by the parable. We probably have more reason to expect the return of Jesus Christ than any other generation that has ever lived, but we also have more need than any other generation to not have an *escapist* or *alarmist* attitude. We must serve, we must be mature, we must be strong, we must be patient, and we must raise up the next generation to mightily serve God!

Now, as we enter the midnight hour of the third watch, we might ask ourselves what earthly events give us an understanding of God's clock? What, if any, biblical prophecies still remain to be fulfilled before the Lord comes again? Many Christians try to determine what God uses as a clock to count down the celestial moments until the second return of Christ. Some think that He is bound to wait until the fulfillment of certain prophecies (Acts 3:19-21), while others maintain that His coming is imminent, at any moment, and with nothing restraining Him (1 Corinthians 15:52).

To my way of thinking, the Great Watchman's clock is a combination of many gears and mechanisms that all turn slowly and precisely, together making up the whole perfect instrument used for His timepiece. The rebirth of the nation of Israel, as foretold in Scripture, would certainly appear to be one of the gears on His clock (Deuteronomy 30:1-6). His patience in wanting to give all men a chance to repent and be saved is another (1 Timothy 2:4; 2 Peter 3:10). I would add to this the current missionary efforts to take the gospel to all of the unreached nations of the world as a fulfillment of Matthew 24:14 and 28:19.

Personally, I think the restoration of truth to the church in regard to faith, water baptism, Bible reading, healing, fivefold ministry, spiritual government, praise and worship, the baptism and gifts of the Holy Spirit, intercessory prayer, as well as other restoration truths, is also one of the major components in God's clock. Consider the following passage:

> Repent therefore and be converted, that your sins may be blotted out, so that times of refreshing may come from the presence of the Lord, and that He may send Jesus Christ, who was preached to you before, *whom heaven must receive until the times of restoration of all things,* which God has spoken by the mouth of all His holy prophets since the world began
> Acts 3:19-21, emphasis added

We enjoy the restoration of many scriptural truths today that were not a part of Christian living even one hundred years ago. How many more truths must be restored, and what portion of the global church must be influenced by the "restoration of all things" in order for this to be fulfilled, is a matter of speculation and debate.

I am sure that there are other components to God's Great Clock as well. There is the unity of the worldwide church that Jesus prayed for (John 17:20-26) and the unity of the faith that Paul mentioned in Ephesians 4:13. What this unity of the faith means to God is debatable.

There is also the evil in the world, and the perilous times that Paul preached in 2 Timothy 3:1-9 would be another. Then there are the unfolding of natural signs, such as an increase of volcanic eruptions, earthquakes, destructive weather patterns, and bizarre astronomical phenomenon that many see as a precursor or fulfillment of Matthew 24:29 or Revelation 8:5. Finally, the powerful movement of the Holy Spirit throughout the United States and third world and other countries is not coincidental. God has designed these events for the building up of His church.

Waiting and Watching

Have you ever stood on a busy street corner waiting for a ride? The person picking you up left written instructions for you concerning where you were to meet him and the approximate time. It would be important for you not to go wondering off or get too interested in nearby shops because of not being sure of the time your ride would show up. Occasionally, you glance at your timepiece. Although you're not sure of the vehicle the man is driving, you are confident that you will see him or he will see you if you are in the place he told you to be. All you can do is simply watch and be patient. This is not to say that you can't have a conversation with those around you or enjoy the sights and sounds from where you wait. Yet, there is a desire to be ready because when your ride arrives, you expect the meeting to be a wonderful occasion filled with glorious joy.

One day our ride will arrive; the Lord Jesus Christ will return. There are scoffers who say He will not come (2 Peter 3:4), others who say that Christ already returned (Matthew 24:24), and there are those who say that the resurrection is already past (2 Timothy 2:17-18). But they are wrong! When Jesus comes again, it will be a momentous worldwide event and everyone will know of it.

The Bible says He will return physically (Acts 1:11). Every eye will see Him (Revelation 1:7). He will come with great power and glory (Mark 13:26). The resurrection will occur (1 Corinthians 15:42-58) and there will be a catching up of the saints into the clouds to meet the Lord in the air (1 Thessalonians 4:16-17). Those who have refused the Lord Jesus will be judged, and those who have accepted Him will be justified. Most of the world will be caught off guard by His return because they do not serve nor watch for Him. He will come like a thief in the night.

As servants of the third watch, we have the responsibility to serve our Master and wait for His return. He has told us that He will return. The first and second watches are gone and the third watch is upon us. It is the midnight hour. He may come soon, and when He does, He will bless those servants who watchfully wait for His return. Let us be faithful and humble servants of our Lord and press on into the watch like never before.

> Let your waist be girded and your lamps burning; and you yourselves be like men who wait for their master, when he will return from the wedding, that when he comes and knocks they may open to him immediately. Blessed are those servants whom the master, when he comes, will find watching. Assuredly, I say to you that he will gird himself and have them sit down to eat, and will come and serve them. And if he should come in the second watch, or come in the third watch, and find them so, blessed are those servants
>
> Luke 12:35-38

CHAPTER TEN

QUESTIONS: FOR STUDY, REVIEW AND DISCUSSION

1. Who is drawn to the light of Christianity? What is our role as Christians to those who are in spiritual darkness? How should we approach them?

2. Do you believe that there are angels watching over your life? What does Psalm 91:11-12 mean when it says the angels are there "to keep you in your ways"? Have you ever felt the protection of guardian angels?

3. In the fourth chapter of Daniel we read about the "watchers" who are angels. They brought a certain decree of judgment upon the king. Discuss the concept of watching angels. Have you ever thought of them in this regard before—as heavenly beings that watch your every action and thought? How do these things apply to us today?

4. Consider the Great Watchman's clock. What are some of the things happening in the Church and in the world today that could possibly be components in His clock? Are there others you personally believe which are not mentioned in the chapter?

5. What do you think it will be like when the Lord returns again?

THE THIRD WATCH

A new day is dawning, in the darkest of night
But we enter with joy, for we are the light.
The watchman he hears, and he calls out the hour.
But wait, shouldn't we be up in that tower?

He said to keep watch, for we don't know the hour.
And pray without ceasing, in the cover of the tower.
And be wise and have our lamps filled with oil.
To light up the night, though it seems so much toil.

Off in the east a dark storm, this I saw.
So tell them the good news, don't tell them the law.
The good news is Jesus, the one who did it all.
And through Him, like the mountains, the darkness will
fall.

So turn to Him for the hour is late.
Turn to Him from your strife and hate.
And join hands with God's Army all across the land.
To see the kingdom come, it's right in your hand.

And as the new day dawns, we may hear the trumpet
sound.
And stand before the throne and watch grace abound.
A palm leaf we hold, and adorned in white.
A multitude that helped turn the world into light.

Excerpt from a poem, written by Phil Melior

CPSIA information can be obtained
at www.ICGtesting.com
Printed in the USA
BVHW061938030322
630476BV00006B/878